The Book of Saints

Michael Walsh

TWENTY-THIRD PUBLICATIONS
Mystic, Connecticut 06355

First published in the United Kingdom
by Geoffrey Chapman, A Cassell imprint, London

Reprinted 1995

Twenty-Third Publications
185 Willow St.
P.O. Box 180
Mystic CT 06355
(203) 536-2611
(800) 321-0411

Some of the pieces in this book first appeared in *The Universe* and are used by permission.

ISBN 0-89622-628-X

Illustrations by Sister Elizabeth CSCL
Cover: *The Coronation of the Virgin* by Fra Angelico
(The Louvre, Paris)

Printed and bound in Great Britain by
Mackays of Chatham PLC, Chatham, Kent

Three years ago the editor of the Catholic weekly, *The Universe*, invited me to write a brief feature every other week about the life of a saint. The only provisos were that each saint would be illustrated (which restricted my choices) and that his or her feast should fall within the week following the publication of the brief biography. These fifty-two lives appeared in *The Universe* over the past two years.

It should have been a simple exercise to choose them. There are some ten thousand men, women and children who are listed by name among the people publicly recognized by the Church as saints. At least three-quarters, however, come from the first twelve hundred years of Christianity, before the process of creating saints had been taken over by the Bishop of Rome. During that time people with a reputation for holiness had been publicly venerated in the locality from which they came. Their fame, and especially their reputation for being able to perform miracles, gradually spread until their feast days came to be recorded in 'martyrologies' – lists of saints chronologically arranged according to the day of their deaths. The day of death was generally chosen for their feast because it was the day on which they were 'born' into heaven (the *dies natalis*, or 'birthday'). So although there is a record of a saint's (supposed) day of death, and of the place in which he or she was originally venerated, quite often, very little else is known about them: St George, the patron saint of England, is a good example of this.

So the number of saints from those whose lives it is possible to choose was more limited than it might have seemed at first sight. An added difficulty has been that, over the centuries, feast days had been altered from the day of death for a variety of reasons. In 1969 they were put back again to the *dies natalis* with one or two exceptions such as St Benedict, whose feast day would otherwise fall inevitably during Lent – to the distinct inconvenience of all those monks who follow his rule of life. As yet there is no new martyrology which lists all the new feasts chronologically, and searching out feasts for a particular week proved a time-consuming undertaking.

These considerations apart, I attempted to select saints whose lives illustrated the many and varied aspects of holiness within the Church. There are more men than women, but that reflects the number of saints in general in the Church's calendar. Most of them are monks, or other forms of ecclesiastics, but that, too, is typical. Pope John Paul II has given the Congregation for the Causes of Saints, the body in Rome which proposes people to the Pope for canonization, the task of finding more lay people, and especially more women, to be included among the saints. It will however be a long time before the make-up of the Church's calendar of saints changes very much. The process of declaring someone to be a saint is slow. Each candidate's life and writings have to be minutely examined and, except in the case of those who have died for their faith, there has to be evidence of a miracle attributable to the candidate's intercession with God for each of the two stages, beatification first, and then canonization.

By chance, the book opens and closes with the lives of two American saints – though Frances Xavier Cabrini was born in Italy, her apostolate was very largely in the United States and she died in Chicago. Both are fairly recent saints. I have included lives from modern times, and from the earliest years of Christianity. There are founders of religious orders and church reformers; there are missionaries who travelled round the world and there is an anchorite who spent her life walled into a cell attached to the side of a church in Norwich. There is a Polish saint who was a painter, and another Polish saint who died in Auschwitz. One thing I have learnt from writing these lives: there is no single pattern to sanctity, no especially privileged way to achieving that intimacy with God which is a necessary condition for becoming a saint. **Michael Walsh**

CONTENTS

Contents

St

LIZABETH SETON Over the centuries, many thousands of people have been given the title of 'saint', but the overwhelming majority of them come from the first millennium of Christianity, long before the formal process of canonization controlled by the Pope and his Curia had come into being. Since then the number of holy men and women officially recognized by the Church as saints has fallen dramatically – especially after the establishment at the end of the sixteenth century of a Roman Congregation to oversee the making of them.

As a result there are few saints who come from the 'New World', from North and South America, and in particular very few indeed from the United States, where the predominant religion has not been Roman Catholicism. The first person born in the United States to have been canonized was Elizabeth Bayley Seton, proclaimed a saint by Pope Paul VI in 1975.

She was born in the city of New York on 28 August 1774. Her father Richard was a doctor, and a professor at what eventually became Columbia University. Her mother was Catherine Charlton Bayley, and Catherine's father was a minister of the Episcopal church on Staten Island. Catherine died when Elizabeth was quite young, but the daughter was carefully, and piously, educated by her father.

At the age of eighteen she married William Seton, a prosperous merchant, and in their nine years of marriage they had five children who were, in their turn, devoutly brought up. Unhappily for the family, the international trade in which William was engaged was not flourishing. Between 1802 and 1803 his business collapsed, which brought about a rapid deterioration of his health. To restore it, business acquaintances of William, Antonio and Filippo Filicchi, suggested a visit to Italy.

1

Elizabeth and William, with their eldest daughter, arrived in Leghorn in November 1803, but only six weeks later William died in Pisa. Elizabeth did not return home immediately. She stayed on in Leghorn with the Filicchi family, who were devout Catholics. Filippo had married into a Boston family, and could speak English. From him in particular Elizabeth began to understand something of the Catholic faith and found herself deeply attracted to it. So much so that when she returned to New York the following May she announced her intention of becoming a Catholic. Her Episcopal family and friends were deeply distressed.

They tried to dissuade her, but did not succeed: she was received into the Catholic Church in New York, along with her children, in May 1805. Cut off from her family and from many of her friends by this act, for the next four years or so Elizabeth led an extremely hard life, even though the Filicchi family continued to support her financially. For a time she even moved to Canada, where she hoped to find a more sympathetic culture.

But then, in August 1807, came an invitation to take charge of a school for girls that was to be founded in Baltimore near the diocesan seminary. Elizabeth did not go there until June the following year, but in Baltimore she discovered the vocation which was to be her inspiration for the rest of her life. For not only did she open a school, but she founded an order of nuns – they came to be the American Sisters of Charity – with seven of the young women who were attracted by Elizabeth to work in the school. A year after it began, the school moved to Emmitsburg in Maryland, henceforth the headquarters of the religious congregation Elizabeth had created.

It was an important time in the history of American Catholicism, for the movement to establish parochial schools was just beginning. Not only were Elizabeth's nuns able to

2

staff such schools, under her direction they began to write textbooks for them, and to translate from French spiritual books to feed the devotion of the American Church: Mother Seton wrote some of these devotional works herself.

Education of girls was her chief apostolate, but even in her early youth, before her marriage to William, she had been concerned with the needs of the poor and the sick. From Emmitsburg she ministered in the surrounding countryside to those in poverty or ill-health. She was especially involved with the plight of poor black families, many of whom were received into the Catholic Church as a result of her work on their behalf.

Elizabeth died on 4 January 1821. At her death there were some forty nuns in her congregation, and there were, in addition to Emmitsburg, two other houses, both orphanages, in Philadelphia and New York. Today the congregation she founded numbers thousands of nuns, at work around the world. They, and the Catholic Church in the United States, honour her memory on the commemoration of her death, 4 January.

12 January

ILRED OF RIEVAULX When Ailred first saw the Yorkshire Abbey of Rievaulx in 1134 it was not the building whose graceful ruins now so delight curious tourists. That monastery was constructed nearly a century after the saint's death. Yet he, too, was there as a tourist. He was visiting Yorkshire on an errand to Archbishop Thurstan of York, sent by King David of Scotland to whom Ailred was deeply attached. After meeting the archbishop, Ailred was on his way, possibly, to call on another old friend, Waldef, who had been a boyhood companion at the King's court but was now prior of the canons at Kirkham – and was later himself to become a Cistercian. Ailred spent the night in the castle of the man who had founded Rievaulx two years before, so it was natural that he should ride out the following morning to see the monks in their white woollen habits, who had only recently arrived in Britain from Clairvaux. Perhaps what attracted him was the setting in the valley of the river Rye, a 'second paradise of wooded delight' as Walter Daniel, his friend, disciple and first biographer, described it. He went back to Helmsley that evening, but the following day asked whether anyone in the party wished to make a second visit. One other did: they rode back, and both stayed. King David's emissaries had to return to Scotland without them.

Scotland had not, in any case, been Ailred's home. He was born in Hexham, in 1110. His father was priest there as his grandfather had been, though his grandfather arrived only after a Norman bishop had ousted the respectably married secular clergy from Durham, and brought in monks. The family was distinguished, sufficiently so for Ailred to be sent to the Scottish King's court for his education when some twelve years old. He remained there, eventually achieving

4

office of some sort: there is a suggestion that he looked after the domestic arrangements as seneschal, for in later life he displayed considerable knowledge about feasting.

Like his friend Waldef, King David's stepson, he early felt a call to the priesthood. It was his affection for those around the King, and for one of them in particular, that made him hesitate. His decision after seeing Rievaulx was as firm as it was sudden. He spent four days in the monastery's guest house as custom required, and then joined the novices.

Later on he became master of novices, though only briefly. In 1143, soon after a journey to Rome to represent the monastery's interests at the papal court, he was appointed abbot of a new foundation at Revesby in Lincolnshire. Four years after that he was back in Rievaulx, now as its abbot, and remained abbot until his death in 1167. Not that he could stay long at Rievaulx at any one time. When Ailred joined the community there seem to have been three hundred monks; at his death there were one hundred and forty choir monks and no less than five hundred lay brothers. To cope with such numbers daughter houses were founded. Ailred had to travel between them as visitor, and attend annual general chapters of the Order at Cîteaux.

Yet despite his many travels and, in the last decade of his life particularly, despite his ill health, he managed to write – lives of the saints of Hexham and of King Edward the Confessor, and treatises of spiritual direction, such as *The Mirror of Charity*, and another on *Spiritual Friendship*. There were sermons and a charming little treatise on *Jesus as a Boy of Twelve*, but it was the work on friendship which was most characteristic of the saint.

He believed there was no greater happiness than to love and be loved, but above all to love, and to be loved by God. This conviction he carried with him into the religious life: his affection for the monks over whom he had charge is clear from his writings, as also his fondness for the friends of his childhood and youth, and for his family in Hexham. He called himself 'friendship's child'. Yet despite this sensitivity, and despite the delicacy of his health, he lived an austere life in the most austere of religious congregations. Though crippled with arthritis and other illness for much of the later part of his life, so ill that he had to live in a shed built alongside the monastic infirmary, he continued to observe all the rigours of the Cistercian rule until a year or so before his death.

He died on 12 January 1167, and was buried in the Chapter House, though his remains were later moved to the abbey church. He was never formally canonized, but was venerated in the north of England, and by the Cistercians.

Ailred's prayer for his monks

Thou knowest my heart, Lord, and that whatsoever thou hast given to thy servant I desire to spend wholly on them and to consume it all in their service. Grant unto me then, O Lord my God, that thine eyes may be opened upon them day and night. Tenderly spread thy wings to protect them. Stretch forth thy holy right hand to bless them. Pour into their hearts thy Holy Spirit who may abide with them while they pray to refresh them with devout compunction, to stimulate them with hope, to make them humble with fear and to inflame them with charity. May he, the kind consoler, succour them in temptation and help their weakness in all the trials and tribulations of this life.

14 January

St Saba

SABA While there are many factors behind the unhappy conflict which has torn apart the former Yugoslavia, religion is one of the most significant: the Croats are Catholics, the Serbs Orthodox. Yet St Saba, who is called the Archbishop of the Serbs and who is credited with founding the independent Serbian Orthodox Church, is honoured by both sides.

He was born in 1174 or 1175, the third son of Prince Stephen Nemanja and his wife Anna. He was a pious child, and little interested in affairs of state, even though when he was barely sixteen his father gave him a small region of his domain to govern. When he was seventeen he abandoned it all and, without his parents' knowledge, fled to Mount Athos and joined a Russian monastery. There, along with the monastic habit, he took the name of Saba after the founder of Palestinian monasticism, St Saba the Great. Shortly afterwards he moved to a Greek monastery and began to learn Greek and to read the rich religious literature of the Byzantine Church.

His family begged him to return. They offered bribes – vast amounts of money either for himself or for the monasteries on Athos if only he would come home. He steadfastly refused to do so, and his constancy won over his father. In 1196 Prince Stephen abdicated, took the name Simeon, and himself became a monk – for the first two years in Serbia, but after that on Athos alongside his son.

Simeon did not make the journey alone: many Serbian noblemen and their servants followed him to Athos. It was more sensible that the Serbs should establish their own religious house than live among the Greeks. With the permission of the Emperor in Constantinople they took over the monastery of Khilandri. Saba drew up a rule for them, written in Serbian. About the year 1200 Simeon died, and Saba was ordained a priest.

The siege and fall of Constantinople changed the fortunes of the community. Saba's brother, Prince Stephen II, asked him to return, which he did, bringing with him the relics of his father. He established himself in the monastery of Studenica, and from there with small bands of monks began to evangelize the countryside: the faith of the people, though nominally Christian, was still mixed with heathen beliefs and practices.

The two brothers, Saba and Stephen, fell out in 1216. Saba went back to Athos, while Stephen courted the powers of Western Christendom: he married a daughter of the all-powerful Doge of Venice and received a crown from a papal legate. Saba, on the other hand, turned again to the Emperor of the East, by this time in exile. He visited him at Nicaea in 1219, and was consecrated Archbishop of the Serbs by the Patriarch there. This was the beginning of the independent ('autocephalous') Serbian Church. There were protests by the Archbishop of Ohrid, who believed he had jurisdiction over Serbia, but they were ignored.

Saba returned home with copies of Serbian texts he had written for the community. He finally established himself as archbishop at Zica, one of the foundations he had made during his first return home.

His task now was to reform his church. He set up seven new bishoprics and called a synod of his clergy. Though the Serbians gave at least nominal primacy to the Patriarch of Constantinople, naming him first in the liturgy, Saba kept up good relations with the see of Rome. He informed the Pope of his consecration, and received letters, and another crown, in return. The crown Saba placed upon his brother's head.

His last years Saba devoted partly to maintaining the independence of Serbia – he went on diplomatic missions at his brother's request – and partly to ensuring the independence of his church. In 1229 he went to the East, visiting the Holy Land, and the exiled Emperor. He returned home to find Serbian independence gone, and the country subjected to the authority of the King of the Bulgars.

In 1233 Saba resigned his office as archbishop, and put one of his followers in his place. Then he set off once more on a long tour of the East, back to the Holy Places, off to Alexandria to visit the Patriarch, on to the Thebaid and to Sinai to meet monks; to Constantinople, which was still under Latin control. In the winter of 1234 he went to the Bulgarian capital. There he died, on 14 January 1235. His body lay in the city for a year. Then Serbian monks took his bones back to the monastery of Mjlesevo where, in 1594, the relics were deliberately burned by the Turkish authorities. To the Serbs he is known as St Saba the Enlightener.

St F RANCIS DE SALES Of all the books which have helped Christians in their search for closer union with God, few have been more important, and more widely read, than the *Introduction to the Devout Life*, which appeared first at the very end of 1608, and the *Treatise on the Love of God*, published in 1616. They are complementary, the first being for beginners, the second for those more advanced. Both were written by Francis de Sales, a saint who, from the number of his publications, was declared by Pope Pius XI to be the patron of all authors.

He was born on 21 August 1567, the oldest of thirteen children. His family was noble, and he was born in the chateau de Sales, though his family name was de Boisy. He went to school in Annecy and then, at the age of fourteen, to the University of Paris, where he lived in the Jesuit college. He stayed in Paris for six years, studying rhetoric and philosophy, though he also found time for scripture and theology.

It was towards the end of his time in Paris, when he was nineteen, that the event occurred which set the tone for his devotional life and for the spiritual teaching he passed on to others. When Francis was born the Calvinist belief that people were predestined by God for heaven or hell, and the greater part of the human race was predestined for hell, had also affected Catholics. Francis was no exception. He feared that he had lost God's friendship and that he would be damned for all eternity. He fell into a despair so deep that his health began to suffer. One day, in this anguish, he prayed that, whether or not he were to be damned, he would never give in to cursing or blaspheming. Shortly afterwards, when he was kneeling before a statue of the Virgin Mary and saying the prayer which begins 'Remember, O most loving Virgin Mary ...', the despair left him, never to return. He became overwhelmingly conscious that God wished, not the damnation of all except a handful, but exactly the opposite, that God wanted the salvation of everybody.

There were others of the period who said the same. What was different about Francis was that he wrote down his advice in a manner which was intensely personal. The books, though distributed widely, were originally composed as advice to particular friends of the saint. It was that sense of friendship in his writings on the devout life that made the books so effective.

They were published when Francis was already Bishop of Geneva, but first he had a long struggle to persuade his father to let him become a priest. Francis de Boisy's ambition for his eldest child was that he should enter the service of the state, and so he sent him to Padua to study law: he received his doctorate in 1591. His father now wanted him to marry, but a cousin, Louis de Sales, managed to have him appointed provost of the church of St Peter in Geneva, a sufficiently high position to mollify Francis' father. Francis was ordained in December 1593.

The following year Francis and Louis started out what became a four-year campaign to reconvert from Calvinism the part of the Savoy known as Chablais. They preached, held public debates, started Catholic schools, helped to re-staff parishes and wrote innumerable pamphlets – at least Francis did – against Calvinist doctrine. They eventually won the support of the local Duke and their work was done.

In 1602 Francis was consecrated Bishop of Geneva and he began a new task, reforming his diocese in accordance with the decisions of the Council of Trent. Trent had said there ought to be seminaries for the training of priests. That proved impossible in Geneva, but Francis undertook to do the training himself, conducting examinations and writing a book on how to hear confessions. He was equally concerned that lay people should learn the faith. There was instruction on the catechism in parishes every Sunday, and he established a lay confraternity to teach Christian doctrine.

He also wanted to found an order of nuns who would engage in works of charity outside their convents, and in Jane Frances de Chantal, a widow, he found the perfect person to help him. He first met her in 1604, and became her spiritual director. The first convent of the Order of the Visitation was established at Annecy in 1610, but when the second one was founded at Lyons the Cardinal Archbishop insisted, and Francis complied, that the nuns be restricted to the house as was the requirement of the time, and charitable works outside it became impossible.

Francis died on 28 December 1622 in Lyons, but his body was taken to Annecy and buried there in the church of the Visitation. He was canonized in 1665 and declared a doctor of the Church in 1877. His feast day is now celebrated on 24 January.

A prayer in adversity

> God, thou art my God; I trust myself to thee. Thou art my help, my refuge, and I will fear nothing, for thou art not only beside me, thou art in me and I in thee.

27 January

NGELA MERICI Countless thousands the world over have attended schools run by nuns whose congregation was founded by St Angela. This was the first teaching order of women, and its founder placed it under the protection of the fourth-century martyr St Ursula who had, in regular visions, encouraged the enterprise. She was, in medieval times, venerated both as a patron of universities and as a leader among women.

Angela was born on 21 March 1474 in Desenzano, on the shore of Lake Garda in northern Italy: a town then in the territory of the Republic of Venice. When she was fifteen both her parents died. She went to live with her sister, under the protection of an uncle, at Salò, but soon afterwards her sister died. She was anxious about her sister's salvation, and shortly after her death Angela was granted a vision, the first of many, assuring her that her sister was in heaven. In gratitude Angela, always a devout girl, became a Franciscan tertiary and attempted to live a life of poverty in imitation of St Francis, though without entering a convent.

Next her uncle died, and at the age of twenty she returned to Desenzano. In her native town she saw with new eyes the poverty and ignorance in which so many were forced to live. She determined to improve the condition of the children at least by instructing them. She gathered about her a small group of women, most Franciscan tertiaries like herself, and together they began to teach. The first school in Desenzano flourished. In 1516 Angela was invited to Brescia to begin another, and that succeeded likewise.

Angela travelled. She visited the shrines of Italy. She went to the Holy Land on pilgrimage. In 1525 she went to Rome. She met Pope Clement VII who asked her to transfer herself and her work to Rome. She refused, and went back to Brescia.

By this time she was considering a more formal structure for those who worked with her. She was in part inspired by yet another vision. This time she saw a ladder reaching the heavens with young girls climbing it, each accompanied by an angel. Among them she recognized a friend who had died not long before, and who, in the vision, encouraged her to establish a community of teachers.

Angela and her first companions were not nuns. If they had been, they would have been obliged to wear a distinctive form of dress, say Divine Office in common, and live in enclosed convents, all of which would have interfered with their work with poor children and the sick. Instead they wore simple dresses – black was recommended – and often enough lived with their families.

In 1533 she selected twelve women from the many associated with her to live with her at a house in Brescia. They began a form of noviceship, two years of intense spiritual training. On 25 November 1535 they together (by that time there were twenty-eight of them) dedicated themselves to God, to teaching, and to other works of charity. That day is kept as the foundation date of the Ursulines though Angela's companions were not then, nor were ever in her lifetime, members of a religious order. They did not take vows, nor necessarily live in a community though some did so, or wear a particular form of habit. They did, however, share a common rule of life. It was drawn up for them by Angela, and was initially approved in 1536. The following year she was elected Superior General of her association, and spent the remaining years of her life in the spiritual formation of her growing band of followers.

Early in January 1540 she was taken ill, and died on the 27th of that month. The congregation she founded played an important part in the reform of the Church after the Council of Trent, but it was not allowed to survive as the loose alliance of devout women which she had established: it was forced to become a more traditional form of religious community.

6 February

PAUL MIKI The city of Nagasaki in Japan is now infamous for the devastation caused by the dropping of the atomic bomb upon it in 1945. But it had been revered by Christians in Japan since 1597 because of the deaths there, on 'the holy hill', of twenty-six priests and lay people, the first martyrs of the Japanese Church. They died by crucifixion like their Master, being tied to the crosses as they lay upon the ground and then, when the crosses were set upright, planted in the ground alongside each other, they were put to death by the thrust of a lance, each by a separate executioner.

Christianity came to Japan with Francis Xavier in 1549. By the time he left in the hope of going to China there had been some two thousand converts. After his departure the numbers had continued to grown rapidly, partly at least because of the conversion of a group of the feudal lords who, for reasons of their own, were opposed to the power of the Buddhist monks. Perhaps the great growth in Christianity alarmed Hideyoshi, the ruler who ordered the persecution. Some of the incoming missionaries had little understanding of the particular situation in Japan; the Jesuit superior in the country was, to say the least, imprudent; and the Japanese had a very real fear of invasion by Portuguese soldiers. For these and several other reasons, partly religious, partly to do with the internal politics of Japan, Hideyoshi first ordered the destruction of some churches and other foundations, and then condemned the Christians to death.

Of the twenty-six who died in 1597 six were Franciscans, one of whom was born in India, another in Mexico City; the rest came from Spain. Three were Jesuits, all Japanese, and there were seventeen Japanese laymen. Collectively they are known as Paul Miki and Companions – Paul Miki was a Jesuit priest.

Paul, born in 1556, came from a noble family in Kyoto which converted to Christianity; he was baptized when he was five years old. He went to the Jesuit-run seminary at Anzuciana when he was twenty, but two years later entered the Jesuit noviceship. Though the Jesuits had attempted to adapt the faith to fit in with Japanese culture, in many ways they remained incurably European in outlook: Paul had to learn Latin to study theology, and he found it very difficult. But he also spent a great deal of time studying Buddhism, especially in the form it was found in Japan, and that knowledge became invaluable when he was able to preach and to debate with the Buddhist 'bonzes'. His arguments drew many of his fellow-countrymen and women into accepting the Gospel. It was partly that his sermons were especially persuasive. One Franciscan said of him that he was the most devout of the preachers of the day, and that no one had such great success, but that his success depended at least as much upon Paul's own evident holiness as upon the words which he spoke.

When the persecution broke out Paul was arrested in Osaka, the day after Christmas, 1596. He was imprisoned together with two Japanese Jesuit novices, John Kisai who was sixty-four years old and John Soan de Goto who was not yet twenty: both were received into the Society of Jesus before they were put to death upon their crosses. After their arrest they were taken to Kyoto where each had part of his left ear cut off, and paraded around the city to be scoffed at by the populace. From Kyoto they were sent for execution to Nagasaki, where they died together on 5 February 1597, though their feast is now celebrated by the Church on 6 February.

Of the martyrs who died that day each gave his own example of heroism. St Paul Miki, who had preached so effectively during his life, still on the cross encouraged the many bystanders to embrace Christianity. Just before he died he pardoned those who had put him to death, an act which moved many who heard him. He died saying 'Into your hands, O Lord, I commend my spirit'. John Soan's father was among those who saw the martyrdom. He encouraged his son to endure to the end, saying that both he and John's mother would also willingly die for their faith. This was no empty promise because one of the onlookers who confessed himself a Christian was seized and executed on the spot. One of those who died was only twelve years old; another, Anthony Dojuku, who was thirteen, intoned a hymn.

Many more Christians died in the years which followed, 205 of whom have also been beatified. The twenty-six who were martyred in 1597 were beatified for their heroic witness to the message of the Gospel in 1627, and were canonized by Pope Pius IX in 1862.

St Paul Miki's words to Christians who tried to get him released

> Is that your way of showing your love for me? Did you wish to deprive me of the immense privilege which God has given me? You ought to rejoice, and praise his goodness for it.

14 February

YRIL AND METHODIUS Pope Paul VI proclaimed St Benedict to be patron of Europe. Not long after his election to the papacy John Paul II united the names of Cyril and Methodius to that of Benedict as equally patron saints of Europe. He thereby linked Western Europe, whose culture owed so much to the monks who bore Benedict's name, to Eastern Europe, of which the monks Cyril and Methodius had been the apostles.

They were brothers, Cyril, born around the year 826, being the younger. His family called him Constantine: Cyril was the name he took as a monk. The boys' father was a senior officer in the imperial army, stationed at Thessalonica, and the two grew up speaking the language of the local Slav population. Their father died when Cyril was fourteen years old.

Methodius was also a name in religion: that with which he had been baptized, and the date of his birth, are unknown. Nor is very much known about Methodius' early career, except that, as befitted his status, he was a provincial governor. Cyril went to Constantinople and there studied – brilliantly – philosophy, eventually becoming a professor after being ordained priest and serving for a time as librarian at the great church of Hagia Sophia. He was an important figure in Constantinople, the imperial capital. He vigorously defended the veneration of images – a practice under attack by the Emperor of the day – and also acted as an emissary to a Muslim ruler, in whose court he debated the doctrine of the Trinity. But in November 855 his patron was assassinated. Cyril left the city and became a hermit for a time, before joining his brother in a monastery on Mount Olympus.

Their first missionary journey began at the end of 860,

when they set off with others to the Khazar people in the Caucasus. This was not a particularly successful expedition, but on the way back Cyril discovered in the Crimea some bones which he believed to be those of the Pope St Clement I.

When they returned Methodius became an abbot while Cyril went back to teaching. But not for long. In 862 the ruler of the country which is now Slovakia asked the Emperor in Constantinople for a bishop who could instruct the Slovak peoples in their own tongue. This was not easy, because no alphabet yet existed for that language. Cyril and Methodius invented one, from which is derived the 'Cyrillic' script, and translated the New Testament into it. They also translated the liturgy, but this brought them into conflict with Western-trained clergy who would only accept as sacred (and therefore suitable for the liturgy) Hebrew, Latin and Greek, the three languages used by Pilate for his inscription on the cross.

To resolve the problem, the two brothers set out for Rome with a number of their followers who wanted to be ordained priests, and with the relics of St Clement, which they had carried with them on their missionary journeys. At Rome Pope Adrian II approved their Slavonic version of the liturgy, which was then celebrated in St Peter's. He also ordained Methodius. It was also in Rome that Cyril became a monk and changed his name from Constantine – but died in there only a few weeks later, on 14 February 869. He was buried in the church of San Clemente.

Methodius returned to Slovakia to continue the mission alone. At the end of 869 he was back in Rome to be made an archbishop, with jurisdiction over Slovakia and Moravia. But his authority aroused hostility among some of the bishops of Bavaria, because Methodius' new territory had been formerly under their control. Methodius was not only driven from his archbishopric but was for a time even locked up in a monastery, one of the chief complaints against him being that liturgy in Slavonic was unorthodox.

The saint, however, continued to enjoy the support of the Bishop of Rome, and it was through papal intervention that he was released. His mission prospered despite the many difficulties created by hostile clergy. He even found time, in the midst of a very busy life, to translate the Old Testament into Slavonic (his brother had already translated the Psalms). He also drew up laws, both civil and canonical, in Slavonic for use by the people he had converted to Christianity.

Methodius died on 6 April 885. It was the Tuesday of Holy Week, and the saint was in his cathedral church. That much is certain, but the location of the cathedral is still unknown. The feast day of the two brother saints, missionaries to the Slav peoples, is celebrated on the day on which Cyril died, 14 February.

23 February

St **P**OLYCARP Because the veneration of relics of saints has for so long been part of the devotional life of Catholics, it is hard to realize that this was something quite new to the world in which Christianity grew up. The Romans buried people outside their cities; the Jews feared contamination through the bodies of the dead. Even the author of the Apocalypse says that the martyrs should be left in peace. Despite all this, there is an unambiguous example of veneration for the bones of a martyr very early in the history of Christianity, and the martyr was St Polycarp.

For someone who lived such a long time ago – he was almost certainly born before the year AD 70 – we know a surprising amount about him, partly through Irenaeus, the Bishop of Lyons, who when a boy had heard him preach, and partly through the eyewitness account of his martyrdom. Irenaeus says of Polycarp that he was a disciple of the Apostles, and in particular of St John, and that he was appointed to be head of the church in Smyrna (now Izmir in Turkey, on the Aegean Sea) by John himself. Irenaeus was born no earlier than about 130, so Polycarp must already have been a bishop for thirty years or so when he knew him, and already quite an old man. He heard Polycarp speak of John and of others who had seen Christ, and of what he had learned from them. Years before, Ignatius of Antioch met Polycarp as he was being taken to Rome for his martyrdom. Ignatius had been a particularly vigorous bishop: when he wrote to Polycarp afterwards Ignatius clearly felt that he did not exercise authority as firmly as was proper.

Though Polycarp impressed Irenaeus because of the majesty of his appearance, the saint's letter to the church at Philippi, written in response to a request by Ignatius, reveals a humble, simple man whose Greek was none too good. He knew most of the New Testament well, the writings of Paul, the synoptic Gospels and the Acts of the Apostles, but admitted that he knew little of what we now call the Old Testament. Rather than a philosopher or, like Ignatius, a theologian, he comes across as a pastor of souls. Part of the letter to the Philippians is to do with the problems of the presbyter (priest) Valens and his wife. They had been excommunicated over charges of financial misdoings: with them Polycarp is gentle and compassionate.

But even if no theologian, he had strong feelings on heretics. Irenaeus says that if he heard anything he took to be unorthodox he stopped his ears exclaiming 'Good God! That I should have lived to hear such things'. St Jerome, writing, it is true, long after Polycarp's death, says that when the saint was visiting Rome he encountered the heretic Marcion. It seems that Polycarp tried to avoid him, so Marcion called out 'Do you not know me, Polycarp?' to which Polycarp answered 'I know you as the first-born of Satan'.

That was about the year 154 when he was in Rome to discuss with the bishop there, Anicetus, the date of Easter, which churches in Asia celebrated on a different day from those in the West. The two bishops could not agree on a common date, and decided instead to let the two traditions exist side by side. However, Anicetus was so impressed by his visitor that he asked him to preside at the eucharist in his own church.

It was probably soon afterwards, in 155, that Polycarp met his death in the amphitheatre at Smyrna. When the persecution first broke out his friends prevailed upon him to flee the city, but when eventually caught he surrendered willingly, offered his captors supper, and then spent two hours in prayer. In the place of execution he confessed his faith before the proconsul. 'Blaspheme Christ', said the Roman official, 'and you can go free.' 'I have served Christ for eighty-six years', he replied, 'and he has done me no wrong. How can I blaspheme against my king and saviour?'

He was first ordered to be thrown to the lions, then burnt at the stake. In the end he was killed by a sword, and his body burnt. The Christians gathered together the remains, 'dearer to us than precious stones and finer than gold', said the eye-witness who wrote the account of his martyrdom.

At the spot where the ashes were buried, he went on, 'we will celebrate the anniversary day of his martyrdom, both as a memorial for those who have already fought the contest and to train and prepare those who one day will do so'.

Polycarp's prayer before his martyrdom

Lord, almighty God, Father of your beloved and blessed Son Jesus Christ, through whom we have come to the knowledge of yourself, God of angels, of powers, of all creation, of all the race of saints who live in your sight. I bless you for judging me worthy of this day, this hour, so that in the company of the martyrs I may share the cup of Christ, your anointed one, and so rise again to eternal life in soul and body through the power of the Holy Spirit.

Through Christ be glory to you, together with him and the Holy Spirit, now and for ever. Amen.

27 February

ABRIEL POSSENTI It seems almost to be a rule of the lives of saints that the younger they have died, the more remarkable their early years have been, full of visions and promises for the future. It was not like that with Gabriel Possenti. His was a perfectly normal childhood. He was fond of sport, and especially of hunting. He was particularly taken by the Italian passion for shooting small birds: when his father forbade him to use a gun he became adept with a sling or catapult. He was a reasonably good scholar, but not an over-serious one, and had a liking for the theatre – though he afterwards somewhat blamed himself for it.

He was born in Assisi – and appropriately named Francesco – on 1 March 1838. His family was wealthy, his father being a senior official in the government of the Papal States. His parents were undoubtedly devout, his mother Agnese particularly so. But she, after bearing thirteen children of whom Francesco was the eleventh, died when he was only four. Almost until Agnese's death they had travelled about the Papal States as Signor Possenti's office required. Eventually, however, they settled in Spoleto, and there Francesco went to school, first with the Brothers of the Christian Schools, then with the Jesuits.

From the age of twelve or so he felt himself called to the priesthood. It seems he resisted a little at first, and was encouraged only after recovering from a serious illness. While he was ill a relic of a Jesuit martyr, St Andrew Bobola, was brought to him, which perhaps nourished his belief that his vocation was to the Society of Jesus. He hesitated a little longer, wondering whether the calling was to a more penitential manner of life than that of the Jesuits. He discussed it with a hermit and in the end he entered the Passionists. In that congregation Francesco Possenti received the name by which he is now known, Gabriel of Our Lady of Sorrows, Gabriele dell' Addolorata.

He entered when he was eighteen-and-a-half, on 6 September 1856. A year later he took his vows and ten months after that began his studies for the priesthood. A year later still he was sent to Isola di Gran Sasso, in the Abruzzi, and it was at Isola he died, early in the morning of 27 February 1862. He was then not quite twenty-four years of age, and had received only minor orders.

Little is known of his own thoughts and feelings, and of the graces he received from God during his years as a Passionist, because as he lay dying of tuberculosis he ensured that all his notes and other documents would be destroyed. But in his short life as a religious he was observed by his companions and by his spiritual director, who sometimes made fun of the saint's serious pursuit of perfection. When Gabriel was insistent that he wanted to wear a chain with sharp points next to his skin, his director only permitted him to put it on the outside of his habit so that, as he said 'All may see what a man of great mortification you are'. Gabriel did as he was told, and bore the subsequent mockery in good part.

Doing what he was told was very much part of Gabriel's ceaseless search for holiness. And, as witnesses later testified when his cause was introduced in 1891, it was good that it was. He was always seeking new ways of mortifying himself, and his superiors were just as frequently insisting that he moderate his penances. He obeyed cheerfully, and it is his cheerfulness despite the many sorrows of his life – the death of his mother and of several of his brothers and sisters to whom he was much attached – that is the outstanding mark of his brand of holiness.

His remains were taken in 1892 to the Passionist Retreat of Madonna della Stella near Spoleto. When he was beatified in 1908 his brother Michele was present, and so was the spiritual director who had occasionally poked fun at him. In May 1920 he was canonized, and proclaimed, a few years later, the patron saint of young people who belong to Catholic Action.

HAD The brothers Chad and Cedd were fellow monks and fellow bishops. There had been a family of four sons, all of whom became priests in early seventh-century England. The two were alike: quiet, devout and, above all, patient. It was a time when the rival kingdoms on the island of Britain had to choose between two distinct Christian traditions, the Celtic Christianity they had inherited and that brought more recently from Rome and represented, at the close of Chad's life, by the Greek monk Theodore, Archbishop of Canterbury.

Chad (his name is sometimes and more correctly spelled Ceadda) was younger than Cedd. He was born at the very end of the sixth century. He went to the holy island of Lindisfarne to place himself under the direction of St Aidan, who sent him to Ireland for some of his education in the ways of the spirit. When he came back he was made abbot of the monastery of Lastingham in north Yorkshire which Cedd had founded.

Very little is known about Chad's life, and almost all of what is known comes from one source, St Bede's *History of the English Church and People*, but for most of the time, Chad lived a tranquil, if severe, life as a monk in the Celtic or Irish tradition. But it was the time when Wilfrid was busy spreading in the north of England the new forms of Church practice brought from Rome: the Synod of Whitby, when the pros and cons of the two ways of life were debated, took place in 663/664, and Cedd was an interpreter at this meeting.

The King of Deira appointed Wilfrid as Bishop of York but, because of his attachment to the ways of Rome, Wilfrid went off to the continent of Europe to seek consecration. That was a mistake. While Wilfrid was abroad, the King of

Northumbria appointed Chad in his place. Chad was consecrated by Bishop Wine of the West Saxons, not one of England's most exemplary prelates, aided by two bishops of the Celtic tradition. It was all very doubtful, and when Wilfrid returned in 666 he was, not surprisingly, angry to find he had been replaced in his see. He first withdrew to Ripon, but petitioned the Archbishop of Canterbury, who determined that Wilfrid was rightfully bishop in York rather than Chad. Chad received the decision humbly, and retired back to the monastery at Lastingham.

Perhaps Chad, too, had doubts about his consecration. Shortly after he returned to his old monastery, he was asked by Archbishop Theodore to serve as bishop to the Kingdom of Mercia, in the middle of England. He allowed himself to be consecrated once more, this time according to the Roman tradition, and from Theodore personally he received all the ranks of priesthood.

There were by this time only three years left to him, now as a 'Roman' bishop rather than, as he had been for almost all of his life, a Celtic monk. He threw himself into his new role with enormous apostolic zeal. He made pastoral visits to every part of his new diocese. He faithfully laid down new organizational structures after the scheme proposed by Theodore at the Synod of Hertford. Above all, he moved the centre of his diocese to Lichfield where, according to very doubtful tradition, many thousands of Christians had died in the persecution of the Emperor Maximinian. He built a cathedral and, close beside it, a small monastery, where he lived with a few monks until his death on 2 March 672. There were stories that his brother Cedd, who had died before him, came down from the skies with a choir of angels to escort Bishop Chad's soul to heaven.

He was not forgotten. Many miracles at his intercession were reported and he was promptly revered as a saint. His body was translated into a great tomb in the cathedral he had founded, a tomb which was constantly more embellished as the centuries went by. Though the shrine was destroyed at the Reformation, it is claimed that some of his relics – namely four large bones – were preserved to be re-interred in the Roman Catholic cathedral in Birmingham, which is dedicated to his memory.

OHN OF GOD It is strange how many of those who founded religious orders never meant to. St John of God, however, not only did not intend to found one, he never did so. The Brothers Hospitallers who now bear his name drew up their first rule half-a-dozen years after the saint's death. It was not until 1571 that Pope Pius V formally approved this new religious congregation. Yet in their lives the Brothers Hospitallers encapsulated the spirit of this extraordinary man.

John was born in Portugal, at Montemor-o-novo, in 1495, but for reasons which have never been discovered he was taken from his home at the age of eight. His mother, it is said, died of grief; his father became a Franciscan tertiary.

He went to Spain, where he lived with the family of the steward to Count Francisco Alvarez of Toledo. He worked as a shepherd but, when his proposal of marriage was rejected by the steward's daughter, enlisted in the army. He fought for Spain against the French, and was taken prisoner. Some years after his release he enlisted again and took part in the defence of Vienna against the Turkish armies of Suleiman II.

This second period of military service was shortlived. He was beginning to repent of what he considered his past sins. In 1533 he made a pilgrimage to Santiago de Compostela before again becoming a shepherd, this time near Seville. He was still restless. In 1535 he crossed to Africa, and entered the service of an exiled Portuguese nobleman and his family. They were in great poverty. John worked to support them.

He had wanted to go to Africa, it seems, to care for Christians held there in slavery, and possibly even to suffer martyrdom. But after three years or so he was persuaded that such an ideal was a delusion, and he returned to Gibraltar. There he earned a little money, and with this bought holy

31

pictures and devotional books to sell on the street while, he hoped, engaging his customers in pious conversation. As a tradesman he was a success. In 1538 he moved on to Granada and opened a bookshop.

When Granada was visited by the famous preacher Blessed John of Avila, John went to hear him, and was promptly and dramatically converted. He went about the streets publicly denouncing his sins and doing penance. His behaviour was so odd he was locked up in the Royal Hospital as mentally sick. When John of Avila heard what had been the effects of his preaching he came to visit him. He encouraged him to channel his fervour into something more productive, and St John, after his release from the hospital in October 1538, and after a pilgrimage to Our Lady of Guadalupe, began his apostolate to the sick and to the poor.

First he gathered them in the hall of a house belonging to a nobleman. He then begged enough money to buy a small house, afterwards a larger one. The Archbishop of Granada helped him to enlarge even that to hold the crowds who came to be cared for. Another bishop suggested that he wear a simple habit, and that he add to his name the words 'of God' to indicate he was dedicated to a life of service to the poor, and to the sick.

The hospitals he opened in Granada and later, in 1548, in Toledo, were models of their kind. Each patient had an individual bed; different infirmities were treated in different wards: he has been hailed as the founder of modern hospitals. He had a particular care for the mentally ill, but his charity extended to all in need, to the poor and to the abandoned children of the city. His work flourished, and donations came readily to support it.

In July 1549 a fire broke out in the hospital at Granada. John of God carried out the sick from their beds, apparently passing through the flames unscathed – for which he has been named as patron of firefighters. It was a similar incident, this time a flood, which finally brought about his death. He became ill after saving his pile of wood from a wetting, and a man from being drowned. For a time he managed to hide his growing weakness but eventually had to take to his bed. For a time he was cared for in the home of a wealthy family, but at the last he returned to his hospital. There, on his knees before the altar in the chapel, he died. It was just after midnight, 8 March 1550.

John was declared blessed in 1630, and canonized in 1691. He is naturally a patron saint of those in the medical profession, especially nurses, but in memory of earlier days in Granada and Gibraltar he is also a patron of all engaged in the book trade.

In a vision John heard a voice saying:

> John, all you do for the poor in my name is done for me. It is my hand that receives your alms; it is my body that you clothe, my feet that you wash.

9 March

St

RANCES OF ROME Many cars and buses still have attached to their dashboards or elsewhere medallions or holy pictures of St Christopher, as patron saint of travellers, to safeguard them from harm. But the feast of St Christopher – whose story is wholly legendary – was all but abolished in 1969. If motorists are seeking another patron, the one proposed to them by the Church is St Frances of Rome – who is also the patron saint of widows.

Frances was born in Rome at the beginning of 1384. Her parents were of noble birth and her father, Paolo Bussa de' Leoni, and her brother Simeone both in their turn served in the highest offices of the Roman commune. She had a happy, devout childhood, but it came to a sudden end when she was only thirteen, for she was obliged to marry Lorenzo dei Ponziani. That was a decision of her family: it seems that she would have preferred to become a nun, but that choice was denied her. She left home and went to live in the part of Rome called Trastevere, in a house near the church of St Cecilia, where Lorenzo's brother and his wife also lived. Her first child, a son they named Battista, was born in 1400; there were two other children, Evangelista and Agnes.

It was a difficult time to be living in Rome. In 1378 the college of cardinals had elected one Pope and then changed their mind and elected another within the same year. One of them, Pope Urban VI, remained at Rome; the other, Clement VII, established his court in Avignon and, for a time during Frances' lifetime, there was even a third claimant to the title of Pope. During this time the city of Rome itself suffered greatly. Some of the great buildings fell into ruins; the people departed. Three times between 1404 and 1410 it was occupied by the army of the King of Naples.

All the while Frances and her family stayed in the city.

They were stalwart supporters of the Pope 'of the Roman obedience', and for that loyalty her husband was put into prison – an experience from which he never fully recovered – Battista was taken hostage, their house was sacked by the King of Naples' troops, and the family's property was confiscated. For those who remained in Rome there was the added threat of famine and of the plague. Frances distributed to the poor all the food and wine that the family had, and cared for the sick in several of the city's hospitals, particularly in that of Santa Maria in Cappella, which had been founded through the generosity of her brother-in-law and his wife. Meanwhile there were family tragedies: both Evangelista and Agnes died in 1410.

In 1425, in order to carry out more thoroughly the works of charity which she had been doing among the poor and infirm, Francesca brought together a group of devout women and instituted a society called the Oblates of Mary, based on the church of Santa Maria Nuova in the Forum. They vowed themselves to live as closely as possible to the rule of life of the Olivetan Benedictines under whom Francesca had placed herself for spiritual direction, and whose holiness and wisdom she much admired. The Oblates did not at first live in a convent but in their own houses, keeping as much of the Benedictine rule as they could. In 1433, however, they established a monastery in Rome.

Francesca's husband Lorenzo died in 1435, and the following year she decided to join the community she had been instrumental in founding. For the rest of her life she served as the Oblates' superior, though when she died, on 9 March 1440, she was in her own family home. Because of her compassion for the sick, and the regular sight of her riding around Rome on a donkey distributing alms to the poor, she had become an extremely popular figure in the city, and the cause for her canonization was started right away. She was not declared a saint, however, until 1608, at which time the church of Santa Maria Nuova in which she had been buried was renamed Santa Francesca Romana.

But quite apart from her gentleness and charity, there was another side to her piety. Her parish priest and confessor wrote the story of her spiritual struggles. She was constantly caught up in visions – even visions of the devil tempting her, from which temptations she was defended by a constant vision of her guardian angel at her side. It is perhaps because of this vision of her guardian angel, together with her ability to see in the dark, that she was declared the patron saint of motorists by Pope Pius XI in 1925.

17 March

St P

ATRICK For a saint as well known as Patrick has become, it is astonishing that so little can be learned about his life, but it is clear he was born and lived, until his capture by Irish pirates, on the west coast of Britain. In his *Confession* or autobiography Patrick named his birthplace 'Bannavem Taberniae' but its location cannot now be determined: it could be anywhere between the mouth of the river Severn up to what is now Scotland. His father Calpornius was relatively wealthy. Patrick says that his father was a deacon, and his grandfather a priest. Though clerics, they do not appear to have been particularly devout. Patrick writes that when, at about the age of sixteen, he was taken off to Ireland as a slave, 'I did not then know the true God'.

His conversion came about, he tells us, during the six years he lived and worked as a herdsman in Ireland. He prayed, he says, as many as a hundred prayers a day and just as many at night, in forests and on mountainsides, whether in snow, or frost or rain. The idea that he should escape came to him in a dream: a boat was waiting, he was told, to take him out of the country. He says the ship was two hundred miles off, and he had to walk there. Then, after a dispute with the captain and crew, he was allowed on board and they sailed for three days.

Where the ship landed at the end of the voyage is one of the major uncertainties of Patrick's life. It used to be thought that it was Gaul (France), but on the whole this seems unlikely. It is much more likely that he had come to another part of Britain. He eventually made his way home to be welcomed by his family at Bannavem Taberniae, a man deeply changed by his experiences. He studied for the priesthood, and was ordained. And then his life was changed again by a dream.

This time he saw a man whom he calls Victoricus coming from Ireland. Victoricus had a pile of letters in his hand, and he gave one to Patrick. It was headed 'The cry of the Irish', and was a plea for him to return to evangelize the territory where he had been held captive. Though the dates are uncertain, it is likely that Patrick travelled back to Ireland about the year 435, a bishop-apostle sent by the British Church.

He was not the first, nor the only, apostle of Ireland, but he was the most successful, and the most lovingly remembered. His mission, which seems quickly to have won support from among the Irish kings (he speaks of their sons travelling about with him) was like that of any missioner: preaching, baptizing. He makes an especial mention of combating the worship of the sun god. He chose Armagh, still Ireland's primatial see, as the centre of his activity, and he seems to have organized the Church in the manner already established elsewhere – namely along diocesan lines rather than based on monasteries, which was later the practice in the Celtic Church.

Although he was not a monk himself, it seems most likely that it was Patrick himself who introduced monasticism to Ireland, and he speaks with great reverence of those who choose this ascetic form of life. That suggests he had spent time in Gaul – though it could not have been for a very long period, or his Latin would have been better than it was.

When he came to write his *Confession* he was clearly an old man, apparently living in semi-retirement in Ireland with his life's work accomplished. His spirituality, however, was still deeply affected by his early experience of slavery, except that now his master was Christ. The day of his death, just like the year, is unknown, but his feast has always been kept on 17 March.

St Patrick's Breastplate

I bind unto myself the name,
   The strong name of the Trinity;
By invocation of the same,
   The Three in One and One in Three.
Of whom all nature hath creation;
   Eternal Father, Spirit, Word:
Praise to the Lord of my salvation,
   Salvation is of Christ the Lord.

St J

OHN CLIMACUS Some saints are known by the name of the town in which they were born, some by the name they took when they entered religious life, others, more modern ones, by their surnames just like the rest of us. But one saint has been called after something he wrote. John Climacus means, literally, John of the Ladder, and *The Ladder of Divine Perfection* is the book which made him famous.

The book is better known than the man. Among the many spiritual treatises of Eastern Christianity none has been so widely studied. Every Lent it is the appointed reading for monks in monasteries of the Orthodox Churches, not just in Greece but in Russia and elsewhere. It has been as widely read in the East as the *Imitation of Christ* by Thomas à Kempis has been in the West.

John was born probably around 570 and died about the year 650, but both dates could vary by as much as half a century. His biographer Daniel does not seem to have known him well, if at all. He records that, at the age of sixteen, John came to the desert of Sinai, but he does not say where he came from. There he found the monastery of St Catherine which the Emperor Justinian had fortified and endowed with icons. He stayed, but lived slightly apart from the community.

In the surrounding desert there were small groups of monks living under the guidance of a spiritual master. John decided to put himself into the hands of Abba Martyrius. After three years Martyrius decided that his pupil had advanced far enough to be made a monk, and took him up the 7,500-foot mountain, which Moses had once climbed, to a chapel at the top. There he cropped his hair in the monastic tonsure.

On the way down the two met the abbot of St Catherine's, who prophesied that John would himself one day be abbot.

At that time, however, nothing was further from John's thoughts. After the death of Martyrius he withdrew deeper into solitude, possibly to a spot on the southernmost tip of the Gulf of Suez.

But he could not remain alone for long. The fame of his holiness had spread. Other monks came to seek his advice, so many, says his biographer, that John was accused of being a chatterbox. He promptly refused to talk to anyone at all, a state of affairs which went on for an entire year until those who had criticized him came to beg him break his silence.

His solitary life lasted forty years, though he did break off at least once to visit a huge monastery at Alexandria. This community much impressed him, as did its 'prison' to which monks unfaithful to their calling were committed with mounds of palm leaves to make into mats and baskets. Both the monastery and the prison are described in *The Ladder*.

And then, at the end of the forty years, he was elected abbot of the monastery on Mount Sinai which he had long known but to which he had never belonged. At the meal which marked his installation, says John's biographer, Moses himself came and served the guests. How long John was abbot is, like so much of the rest of his life, uncertain. It seems he was never ordained to the priesthood but remained a layman all his life. Before his death he resigned his office in favour of his brother George, and returned to the solitude he loved to compose his soul.

The Ladder of Divine Perfection was written when he was abbot of St Catherine's at the request of the abbot of another monastery. He was not the first Christian spiritual writer to use the image of a ladder to mark the steps to God, but it was he who made this a standard metaphor of the ascent of the soul. He gave the ladder thirty steps, one for each year of Christ's life before his baptism, his hidden life. But for John, the Christian soul never stops climbing. The end of the ascent is love, and love is a relationship which is always progressing, always growing.

5 April

St JULIANA OF LIÈGE The feast of Corpus Christi is one of the great celebrations of the Church's year, observed the world over with processions and frequently marked by colourful local customs. Yet it is far from being one of the oldest festivals, and it owes its origins to the enthusiasm of one person in particular, Juliana of Liège.

She was born probably somewhere between 1191 and 1193. She and her sister Agnes, orphaned when Juliana was five, were placed in the charge of nuns at Mont Cornillon, a religious house for both men and women, committed to the care of the sick. Agnes died young. In time Juliana herself became a nun, entering the community about the year 1207.

Two years later she had her first vision. It was of a full moon, a little of which was somehow obscured. The image frequently recurred. Twenty years later Christ explained in a another vision what that strange image had meant. The moon stood for the cycle of the Church's feasts. The blemish on the moon was a sign that the full round of feasts was not yet achieved. There was one missing, a feast in honour of the Blessed Sacrament. There was a growing devotion to the eucharist, which increasingly was being venerated outside the context of the mass. It was not surprising that when Juliana revealed her visions there was a swift response from the church people of the city.

Juliana finally gained the courage to speak about her experiences, it seems, from the confidence the nuns at Cornillon had shown in her when, in 1225, she was elected prioress of the community. She mentioned them to her friends among the holy women of the city, and then to John of Lausanne, her confessor. He in turn approached other learned men of the city, and of the University of Paris. The Dominicans of

Liège were especially important in the support which they gave Juliana when she was criticized for her visions.

But for the feast itself her most important advocate proved to be James Pantaleon. He was then an archdeacon within the diocese of Liège but in 1261 he became Pope Urban IV. In 1264, the year he died, Pope Urban made Corpus Christi a feast of the universal Church – the first time a Pope had ever done such a thing. He also commissioned St Thomas Aquinas to write the Office for the feast. By that time, however, the feast was already being celebrated in Liège itself, approved by Bishop Robert in 1246. It was Bishop Robert who fixed the day as the Thursday after Trinity Sunday, which is still the Feast of Corpus Christi.

Bishop Robert died that same year. His successor was neither as favourable to the feast, nor as sympathetic to Juliana. As prioress she had reformed the rule of life at Cornillon to make it more rigorous, and that was unpopular with a number of the community. The new bishop came down on the side of the dissidents, and in May 1248 Juliana was ousted not only from her position, but from the house as well. With a few of her friends from Cornillon she wandered from place to place until she eventually found refuge at the Cistercian house of Fosses.

Juliana spent her last years in poverty, and as a recluse. When she died, on 5 April 1258, she must have believed that her desire to establish a feast in honour of the Blessed Sacrament had come to nothing. Yet it was only half-a-dozen years later, through the efforts of the friends of her youth in Liège, that Pope Urban gave his approval.

Juliana has never formally been canonized, or even beatified. A feast in her honour, however, was granted in 1869.

11 April

St G

EMMA GALGANI Every century since the time of St Francis of Assisi there have been some who have received the stigmata, the marks in their own body of the wounds Christ received in his passion. In the past half-century the best known has been Padre Pio. A century ago it was Gemma Galgani.

Gemma was born near Lucca, on 12 March 1878. Her father was a chemist and the family was relatively rich. Her mother was Aurelia Landi, and the Landis already had one saint in the family. Aurelia was extremely devout, and her piety passed to her daughter. Before Aurelia's death, when Gemma was only seven, the little girl was convinced that God had asked her permission to take her mother from her. The only thing that grieved her was that she could not die too, and go to heaven.

After her mother's death she became seriously ill. When she recovered she committed herself to the service of the poor, begging money from her father, and if that was sometimes not forthcoming, giving those who came to the door in search of alms food or clothing in place of cash. One memory of her mother's illness and last months on earth stuck in her mind. As Aurelia lay in bed, a crucifix was upon her lap: Gemma, even as a child, developed a great devotion to the Passion of Christ, and to his death upon the cross. Early in the year 1896 she prayed to suffer alongside the suffering Jesus. From then on she saw everything that happened to her as a step towards closer union with her Redeemer.

And sufferings came in plenty. In November 1897 her father died after a long illness. His business had long since collapsed, and the family was reduced to poverty. After his death Gemma went to stay with a wealthy aunt, but she was soon back in Lucca. The pretext was another bout of illness: the true reason may have been that there were young men who wanted to marry her. The illness was real, nonetheless. Once again in Lucca she was confined to bed. There she read the life of the Passionist St Gabriel of Our Lady of Sorrows. It moved her deeply, and henceforward she turned to St Gabriel as one of those closest to her.

Her spiritual director at this time, as he had been from her childhood, was Monsignor Volpi, Archbishop of Lucca. He was a no-nonsense sort of priest, highly sceptical of the mystical experiences which Gemma appeared to be having. But he was also a holy man. He suggested that for an improvement in her health she pray to St Margaret Mary Alacocque. She did so, and was cured, she believed, by the person of Christ coming to her sick bed and laying his hands on her. St Margaret Mary was a Visitation nun. Gemma now felt attracted to join the same congregation of nuns, but though she stayed for a while with them her health was not up to it. She had to content herself with spending short periods in convents while making retreats.

Then, in the evening of 8 June 1899, she had a vision of herself standing before Mary, with her guardian angel beside her. After she had made an act of contrition at the command of the angel, Mary told her that her sins had been forgiven. Jesus then appeared. The flames coming from his wounds burnt themselves into Gemma's hands, feet and side. Later the following year she had a vision of Christ crowning her with the crown of thorns: from then on she was frequently in pain from Thursday afternoons until Friday afternoons. A friend saw blood flow from the wounds the crown was making. At times, too, she felt, and bore the wounds, of the scourging. Other visions were more comforting, in the presence of St Gabriel, her guardian angel, of Mary, of Christ. She would speak familiarly to them: people around her bedside took notes of what she said.

In the last months of her life she contracted tuberculosis. Her spiritual adviser instructed that she should leave the household in which she was living to avoid infecting others. She returned to the poverty-stricken home of her aunt, there to die almost in destitution on 11 April 1903. Immediately there sprang up a widespread devotion to Gemma Galgani. Her popularity continued to grow after she was made a saint in 1941, especially so when her letters recounting the strange events of her life were published. But these events were not the reason for her canonization. She was made a saint for her extraordinary piety, for her resignation to the will of God, and for her obedience to the counsels of those who guided her in the ways of the spirit.

21 April

St A NSELM OF CANTERBURY

St Anselm is in fashion. Few saints have in recent years been the subject of so many books. His own writings have been translated and commented upon. They are on the syllabus of university courses. In his day he was a scholar, and was recognized as such by his contemporaries. But above all he was a holy man.

He was born in 1033 at Aosta in northern Italy, into a rich family of minor nobility. He thought of becoming a monk, but decided against. After his mother's death he quarrelled with his father and left home. He never went back even when the opportunity presented itself, as it did a couple of times in later life. But if he had no nostalgia for his home town, the memory of the mountains among which he grew up stayed with him to the end of his days. He talked about them to Eadmer, his faithful disciple and biographer.

Anselm crossed the Alps to France. He told Eadmer little of what happened to him over the next three years, not picking up the story until the point when he was attracted by the reputation of the school at Bec in Normandy, under the great Lanfranc. Bec was a monastery: Anselm was not a monk. For three years he studied and endured the hardships of monastic life which were a necessary accompaniment to the studies. He came to the conclusion that if he had to live like a monk, he might as well be one. He thought of joining the great Abbey of Cluny, but came to the conclusion that the very full round of liturgical observance would get in the way of learning. He stayed at Bec and read St Augustine.

It was not all study. After only three years he was chosen to succeed Lanfranc as prior and then, in 1078, he was elected abbot. The Abbey of Bec had estates in England, and Anselm travelled to them, renewing his acquaintance with Lanfranc, now Archbishop of Canterbury. Once again he made a deep impression on those he met. When Lanfranc died in 1089 Anselm was the popular choice to succeed him.

But the King, William Rufus, would not have Anselm – or anybody. While there was no Archbishop of Canterbury, the King was receiving revenue from Canterbury's estates. So it continued for four years, until William thought he was dying, and agreed to the appointment of Anselm, who happened to be in England at the time. The saint was at first unwilling to accept, but in March 1093 finally did so: obedience to lawful superiors, whether religious or lay, was one of the cornerstones of his spiritual life.

There were limits to that obedience, at least to secular rulers. He opposed the King over the rights of the Church and in 1097 had to go into exile. He used the time to write perhaps the most famous of his books, called *Why Did God Become Man?*, and became a close friend of the Pope.

Under a new King, Henry I, he returned to England, but three years later was again in exile for much the same reasons as before. A compromise between King and Archbishop was achieved at Easter 1106. Anselm returned. He set about reforming the English Church. He held Church councils. He insisted upon celibacy for the clergy. He created the diocese of Ely. But he was old, and he was tired. On 21 April 1107 he died upon a bed of sackcloth and ashes as dawn was breaking. It was Palm Sunday.

In his life Anselm had attracted honours and respect. He had striven for the liberties of the Church as they were then understood. He had been celebrated for his theological learning. His life as monk and archbishop had helped him along the road to holiness, but it was not these alone which had made him a saint.

The evidence of his deep holiness is to be found everywhere in his writings. He composed prayers and meditations.

He wrote letters of advice to novices about how they should obey the rules of their order as a means to advance in perfection. At the same time he told a fellow abbot not to be too hard on the young boys in the monastery: they needed greater freedom if they were to grow up undamaged by the discipline of monastic life. He wrote about the friendship which was the bond in monastic communities, and about humility, even humiliation, as a means to overcome oneself and to become perfect. He was not the first to foster devotion to Our Lady, but before St Bernard he was perhaps the most influential.

Through his holiness and self-denial as a monk and as Archbishop he became a saint, though never formally proclaimed as one. For his writings he was, in 1720, declared a Doctor of the Church.

A prayer of St Anselm

O God, let me know you and love you, so that I may find joy in you; and if I cannot do so fully in this life, let me at least make some progress every day, until at last that knowledge, love and joy come to me in all their plenitude. While I am here on earth let me know you fully; let my love for you grow deeper here, so that there I may love you fully. On earth then I shall have great joy in hope, and in heaven complete joy in the fulfilment of my hope.

He was even accused of murdering a bishop, but was able to produce him alive to confute his accusers. What seems finally to have led to his expulsion from Alexandria by the Emperor was the charge put about by his enemies that he had threatened to stop the corn shipments from Egypt to Rome. This was his first exile. It did not last long: after Constantine's death his successor allowed Athanasius to return. But by that time a new bishop, Gregory of Cappadocia, had been appointed in his place. There were riots in Alexandria as supporters of the rival bishops came into conflict, and Athanasius again went into exile, this time to Rome, where he received the backing of Pope Julius.

Gregory died in 345. Athanasius went back the following year, and ruled his diocese relatively peacefully for a decade. But the Arian controversy smouldered on. When all the world was Arian, it was said, only Athanasius kept the true faith. *Athanasius contra mundum*: Athanasius against the world. It could not last. After a number of condemnations by Church Councils in 356 an attempt was made to arrest him. He only just escaped with his life, and took refuge with his great supporters, the monks of the Egyptian desert.

He was called back to Alexandria by the pagan Emperor Julian, but his intransigence, and his success in persuading others of his anti-Arian views, finally irritated Julian so much that he sent him into exile once more. That was in October 362: in June 363 Julian was killed in battle. Athanasius was again allowed home, but exiled yet again by a pro-Arian Emperor in 365, despite demonstrations in his favour by the people of the city. In 366, however, he was permitted to return, and died peacefully in Alexandria on 2 May 373: his 'birthday into heaven' has been celebrated on that anniversary ever since.

Athanasius may have lived a combative public life, but his earliest Christian aspirations had been to join the ascetics in the Egyptian desert, and to live a life totally dedicated to prayer and penance. He wrote the life of St Anthony, who is regarded as the father of monasticism. When he went to Rome he took two monks with him, introducing to the Western Church a form of life by that time well established in the East.

Although the theme of most of his many writings was determined by his conflict with the Arians, his first major book, *On the Incarnation*, was written about 318, before Arius came to prominence. Nearly seventeen centuries later it is still being studied in theological colleges. He also wrote about the divine nature of the Holy Spirit which, in the wake of the Arian controversy about the divine nature of the Son of God, had also been called into question.

When he came to preach about the life of Athanasius, Gregory of Nazianzus described him as 'gentle, free from anger, sympathetic, sweet in words, sweeter in disposition'. Not all his contemporaries would have agreed with Gregory. But there is no doubt that Athanasius greatly influenced the way the Church thinks about the person of Jesus.

From On the Incarnation

The Word of God, incorporeal, incorruptible and immaterial, came down to our world. Not that he had been far off before, since no part of creation was ever without him. Together with his Father he filled all things.

He came to us full of love for us and showed himself to us openly. He took pity on our race and our weakness and was so moved by the corruption that had got the better of us, that he could not allow death to rule over us any longer.

Bl.

JULIAN OF NORWICH Although Julian is called 'blessed' she has never formally been either beatified or recognized as a saint by the Church. She has, however, long been venerated for the depths of spiritual insight displayed in her *Book of Showings*. Yet despite this lengthy book, any life of Julian of Norwich must necessarily be short. For one thing, not even her name is known for certain: she was an 'anchorite', someone, that is, who was enclosed within the walls of his or her room or cell. In the Middle Ages these cells were frequently attached to the walls of churches. Julian's cell was beside the church of St Julian in Norwich, and it is quite likely that the woman to whom the *Showings* or revelations were granted simply took her name from that of the church. But she was certainly known as Julian: she is mentioned by name in a number of wills of the time – which help to date her life.

Her date of birth is a problem too, and the date of her death is completely unknown. Julian herself says that, at the time of her illness which culminated in the visions she received on 13 May 1373, she was over thirty years old, so it seems she was born early in 1343. What little evidence there is points to Julian still being alive in 1416 – though if a another nun had succeeded her in the same cell, and also taken the name of the church's patron saint, then we have no means at all of knowing anything about her after 1413 when she was consulted by another great English mystical writer, Margery Kempe.

Julian was a nun at the time of her *Showings*, and probably did not become an anchorite until after the book recounting them had been completed. That much we can learn from what she wrote. On the other hand it is not certain where she was a nun. There were many churches and religious houses in and around Norwich, for in the Middle Ages the town was

57

second only to London in wealth and, probably, second only to Lincoln in the number and strength of its religious foundations of various sorts.

One of them was the Benedictine Abbey at Carrow just outside the town walls. It fell to the Abbess of Carrow to appoint the priest to the living of St Julian's church, which suggests that Julian may have been a nun in that house. Wherever it was that she lived, she received an exceptionally good education. Her *Book of Showings* demonstrates that she was a woman of considerable intellectual ability which some scholar had clearly fostered. She knew Latin well, and the Scriptures – she could make her own translations out of the Latin text of St Jerome. She had read the great Christian writers such as Augustine and Gregory, but she had also read spiritual books in English. She was an accomplished writer of English herself, who was able to wear her learning lightly, and use it without pretentiousness.

She calls herself a simple, unlearned woman. She had not, she says, merited the many great graces which had been bestowed upon her. But then no one 'merits' grace: what Julian was saying was simply sound theology. But she was also humble, and unwilling to appear a 'bluestocking' or give offence through her learning. 'The more sorrow and shame and reproof you receive in this world', she told Margery Kempe, 'the more is your merit in the sight of God. You need patience, for in that you will preserve your soul.'

The fact that she was consulted by Margery Kempe (about a private vow of chastity she and her husband had made) indicates that Julian was regarded as a spiritual director of considerable ability.

Her fame certainly extended far beyond Norwich even in her own lifetime. Not that her spiritual teaching was ever as popular as it has become in the twentieth century apart, perhaps, from among the English Benedictine nuns exiled to

France and the Low Countries during the years of persecution. In modern times, however, her book has been constantly in print, and in demand for the commonsensical and (unlike some of the other English mystics) restrained spirituality – including devotion to the wounded heart of Jesus – that it teaches.

Words of Christ from a vision of Julian of Norwich

> 'Thou shalt not be overcome', was said full clearly. . .
> He said not 'Thou shalt not be tempested, thou shalt
> not be travailed, thou shalt not be dis-eased', but he
> said 'Thou shalt not be overcome'.

ICHAEL GARICOÏTS The shrine of Betharram lies nine miles west of Lourdes, beside the same river Gave which flows beneath the grotto which has made Lourdes famous. Betharram is a much older place of worship. It dates from the thirteenth century and its name, 'beautiful branch', recalls the story that a young girl who fell into the Gave was saved from drowning when the Virgin Mary held out to her a branch from a tree, and pulled her to safety.

When the building of the basilica at Lourdes began, the superior of the priests who guarded the shrine at Betharram was among the first to send a donation. He was Michael Garicoïts.

Both Betharram and Lourdes lie in the French part of the Basque country, and Garicoïts is a Basque name. Michael was born on 15 April 1797, the eldest of six children of Arnaud Garicoïts and Gratianne Etcheberry. He was born in Garacotchea: it means 'house on the heights'. On the slopes of the Pyrenees Michael spent much of his childhood tending sheep and, he later recalled, driving off eagles from the new-born lambs.

He went to the village school and did well. His devotion was obvious to all, and the priest wanted to admit him to his first communion at what was then the early age of eleven: his mother objected that he was not yet ready. He was fourteen before, on Trinity Sunday 1811, he was allowed to approach the altar, and by then he had been hired out as a farm labourer in a neighbouring village.

Soon afterwards he returned home to tell his parents he wished to become a priest. It was not simple piety. He was at that time something of a fighter, and certainly tough. He was inspired by the heroic lives of priests who defied the anti-clerical legislation that followed the French Revolution.

His father said the family could not afford it, but his grandmother thought otherwise. She went off to see the dean. The local clergy owed a debt of gratitude to her family, which had given refuge to priests on the run, smuggling them over the border. Now the dean arranged for Michael to go away to school, while earning his keep by working as a servant.

Michael studied and worked as a servant between 1811 and 1823 when he was ordained. His first appointment was as assistant priest at Cambo, near Bayonne. It was a difficult assignment. The parish priest was old and paralysed, the local mayor hostile, the townspeople largely indifferent. By his preaching, by his devotion to the sick and the poor, and by catechizing the young, he began to change attitudes. He started a eucharistic league. More significantly for his later life, perhaps, he started in his parish the Confraternity of the Sacred Heart. Michael's impact upon Cambo was extraordinary, but his stay was short. At the end of 1825 he was sent to Betharram to teach.

In Revolutionary France, the religious orders had been driven out of the country. So Michael had no experience of formal religious life until in 1823 he was appointed confessor to the Daughters of the Cross at Igon. From these nuns, and especially from their founder, St Elisabeth Bichier des Anges, he learned a great deal.

He decided to found a congregation of priests who would be at the service of the local bishop to assist in parishes, teach in schools, lecture in seminaries. He gathered a small group about him, proposing that they should live under a form of Jesuit rule until a formal constitution could be drawn up. The group prospered, though slowly. Schools were opened, including one at Betharram itself. In August 1855 a team was sent to Buenos Aires to serve Basques in Argentina, and the missionary work spread throughout South America.

But in St Michael Garicoïts' own lifetime the Priests of the Sacred Heart of Betharram were not formally established. The local bishop, to whom Michael was always loyal, decided that the priests would remain an informal group of diocesan clergy. It was not until after his death, which occurred on the morning of Ascension Day, 14 May 1863, that his constitution was formally approved.

During his lifetime Michael's devotion to the eucharist and to the Sacred Heart was evident to all; occasionally a seemingly supernatural light shone about him. After his death miracles were reported. But it was not until July 1947 that he was declared a saint, together with his guide in the religious life, Elisabeth Bichier.

22 May

St R

RITA OF CASCIA Among Italians, it has been said, the popularity of devotion to Rita of Cascia is at least as great as devotion to the Blessed Virgin. For them she vies with St Jude as the patron of hopeless cases, perhaps because, in her own life, she triumphed over so many obstacles, most particularly the difficulties of her own marriage.

She was born about the year 1381 in Roccaporena, a small village near the town of Cascia, in the province of Perugia. Even as a little child she developed a great devotion to Christ and made for herself a tiny chapel within her parents' house where she used to spend many hours in solitary prayer. It was hardly surprising, then, that she wanted to become a nun. Her mother and father had other ideas and as she was always an obedient, docile child, she was persuaded to marry a young man of the neighbourhood who had the advantage, in their eyes, of being wealthy. But he was also violent and unfaithful.

All this Rita bore without complaint for eighteen years, though her kindly disposition, gentle obedience to her husband, and goodness to all around succeeded, as time went on, in mitigating her husband's brutality. Nevertheless, he came to a violent end, murdered in a vendetta while on his way back to his house from Cascia. The two sons wished to avenge their father's assassination, as was the custom of the time. Rita prayed that they would not, and looked upon the fact that they died (of natural causes) before they could take their revenge as an answer to her prayers.

With the death of her husband and children she was now free to fulfil her childhood desire to become a nun. She asked to be accepted into the Augustinian convent of St Mary Magdalene in nearby Cascia. At first they would not have her because she was a widow and because she was illiterate. But she remained constant in her request and was eventually admitted thanks, she always believed, to the power of her patron saints, John the Baptist, Nicholas of Tolentino, and Augustine of Hippo. Despite the fact that she could not read, she was permitted to join the choir nuns, saying her own prayers instead of chanting the divine office.

Her piety was remarkable, and aroused the admiration of her fellow nuns. To them she was a constant example of virtue, and above all of devotion to the Passion of Christ, to which she directed all her prayers and meditations. One day, kneeling in prayer before a crucifix, she felt a thorn from Christ's crown of thorns enter her forehead, leaving a deep wound. The wound was obvious to all, and it stayed with her until her death. On one occasion, however, when she was making a pilgrimage to Rome and wished to be able to mingle unremarked with the crowds, she prayed that it might go away for a while, which it did.

Rita's holiness, already well known in Roccaporena, became equally so in Cascia itself. She was venerated as a saint within her own lifetime, and indeed as a miracle worker. When she died of tuberculosis, on 22 May 1447, an angel, it is said, sounded the bell to mark her passing. So great was popular feeling that only ten years after Rita's death the local bishop gave permission for her to be publicly acknowledged as a saint. Her body remained incorrupt, and even survived a fire which destroyed her first simple coffin. Her body was then laid in a much more elaborate sarcophagus, where it remains to the present day.

St J

OAN OF ARC Perhaps it is not so unusual for saints to be reviled during their lifetime by some who knew them, and then praised for their virtues after their death. But there is only one saint burned as a witch in one generation, and then canonized in a much later age. Jeanne la Pucelle – Joan of Arc as she is more commonly known – was sent to the stake on 30 May 1431. On 15 May 1920 Pope Benedict XIV solemnly declared her a saint.

There is no doubt about her holiness of life, even if it was expressed in an extraordinary way. She was born on 6 January 1412 in Domrémy in Champagne. When people who had known her as a child testified about her childhood, they remembered her being prayerful as well as playful, as concerned for the sick and the homeless as she was for the services in her village church.

But this was the time of the Hundred Years War between England and France, with the Burgundians as allies of the English. At least on one occasion Joan had to flee her village as it was ravaged by the troops of the Duke of Burgundy. Then, when she was fourteen, she received her remarkable commission. She saw in a vision a group of saints who told her it was her task to free France of its enemies.

She could not believe it. She was a simple peasant girl, one without learning (she could not read or write) and without contacts at the court of the Dauphin (he had succeeded to the throne of France as Charles VII, but had not yet been crowned). Nonetheless she went to the local commander of the Dauphin's forces to tell him of her voices. He laughed at her, but then changed his mind when a defeat occurred which she had prophesied. He sent her, with an escort, to the royal court. Charles, too, laughed at her, disguising himself so he would not be recognized, but to his amazement Joan saw through this disguise. He sent her off to Poitiers to be examined for orthodoxy by a group of theologians. They found no fault.

Joan had asked for troops to undertake the relief of Orléans: they were now provided, and she rode off to the besieged city. She went dressed as a man, in white armour. Over her army flew an especially made flag with upon it the words 'Jesus Maria'. She entered Orléans on 29 April 1429. By 8 May the English had been defeated, their forts captured, and Joan wounded by an arrow, a fact which considerably increased her prestige among the soldiers.

But there were still those who were unwilling to credit her with the relief of the city. The doubters altered their opinion when shortly afterwards she went with the Duke d'Alençon on a highly successful campaign along the Loire valley. The English army they defeated at Patay was under the command of Sir John Fastolf.

The way was now open to Rheims, the city in which kings of France were crowned. The coronation of Charles VII took place on 17 July 1429, with Joan standing beside him, under her banner.

The war went on, but Charles failed to give Joan the support she needed. The French attempted to take Paris, but Charles did not turn up to spur on his troops. The attack failed and Joan was again wounded and this time nearly captured. She finally fell into the hands of the Burgundians when the governor of the city of Compiègne pulled up the drawbridge too quickly, leaving her trapped outside. The Burgundians sold her to the English.

The English had attributed Joan's remarkable success to witchcraft, and in Rouen on 21 February 1431 put her on trial. The president of the tribunal, the Bishop of Beauvais, was in the pay of the English and selected all the judges. She was questioned about her visions and her voices. She was accused of not being prepared to submit to the authority of the Church. One of the most serious charges was that she had put on men's clothes. She promised to dress as a woman, but when she was returned to her prison cell seems to have changed her mind. She was declared to be a recalcitrant heretic, her voices deemed to be of the devil. The decision was ratified by the University of Paris and she was handed over by the Church to the 'secular arm' – the English army – to be put to death. She was not twenty years old when she died, and to prevent a shrine being erected her ashes were scattered on the Seine. She was declared patron of France in 1922.

St B

ONIFACE   There is a statue of St Boniface in the town of Crediton in Devon. Whether he was born there, about the year 675, is uncertain, as to both place and date, but both are near enough. He was baptized Wynfrith, a name which meant 'joy and peace'. His parents were probably members of the West Saxon nobility: certainly he was related to high-born families. At the age of seven he was placed in a monastery for his education, most likely in the Minster at Exeter. This would have prepared him for a career in either Church or State, but his first inclination was for an academic life. At fourteen he transferred to the Abbey of Nursling to study under its learned Abbot Winbert. He became so expert that Winbert made him director of the school: Wynfrith also composed England's first Latin grammar.

At the age of thirty he was ordained. He continued to teach, but his reputation for learning and holiness had reached beyond the confines of his monastery. The King of Wessex asked him to represent him before the Archbishop of Canterbury.

By now, however, his interests were elsewhere. In 716 he obtained permission from his abbot to preach in Frisia, that area of northern Europe from which some at least of the Saxons had first come to Britain, and where the Northumbrian Willibrord was already at work. He had chosen the wrong moment. Paganism was then in the ascendent, and Wynfrith soon returned to Nursling.

In 717 Winbert died. The monks wanted to elect Wynfrith abbot, but he refused. Instead he set off again. He first went to Rome, where his name was changed by the Pope to Boniface which means 'speaker of Good News', and where he was given the task of preaching to the Germans. He went back to Frisia to work under Willibrord, but after three years travelled to Hesse, the territory he had been assigned by Pope Gregory II. In 722 he returned to Rome to report progress – and to be consecrated bishop.

Back in Germany, and with renewed authority, he continued his preaching: so similar, it appears, was his own language and that of the German peoples that he had no difficulty in making himself understood. And one thing the pagans certainly understood: when on one famous occasion at Geismar he cut down an oak, sacred to pagan deities, there was no retribution. The gods were powerless against the might of the Christians.

In 732 the new Pope, Gregory III, sent Boniface the pallium, the woollen stole which was a symbol both of loyalty to Rome, and of the authority of a metropolitan archbishop. He now had authority to found new dioceses wherever it seemed appropriate, which is what he did. At the end of the decade (738–739) he went back to Rome to discuss the problems of his new churches, and was granted the powers of a papal legate, giving him even greater authority over bishops.

Boniface's writ ran not only in Germany, but in what is now France as well. When he had first been made a bishop, Pope Gregory II had commended him to Charles Martel, who at that time was effectively ruler of the area which is now Germany and France. Charles was a law unto himself, but over his sons Carloman and Pepin Boniface was able to exercise more influence. At his behest both held synods over which Boniface presided to reform the Church. He also presided over the ceremony which made Pepin a king. Whether Pepin was crowned is unclear. Boniface, however, certainly anointed him with oil, for the first time conferring an almost priestly status upon kings. But because it was Boniface who did this, it also asserted the power of the church over the state.

In 747 he became Archbishop of what is now Mainz. Boniface did not relinquish his oversight over the dioceses of Germany and Gaul. He had, however, started his missionary career as a monk, and wherever he went he founded monasteries or convents, often with monks or nuns from England, to ensure that the faith was lived and taught. And in them all he insisted that the Rule of St Benedict, by which he himself regulated his life, should be lived to the full.

Missionary work had been his first love, and towards the end of his life he decided to return again to Frisia. But there, in 754, he was killed, perhaps by a band of thieves, as he waited for some new converts to come for confirmation. His body was taken to Fulda, the most famous of all his monastic foundations. There he still lies, close by his cousin St Leoba whom he had persuaded to leave her convent in Wimbourne to assist in the evangelization of Germany. His life's work spanned England, Italy, France and Germany. Surely no other saint can have played so active a part in forging what is now Europe.

From a letter of St Boniface

In her voyage across the ocean of this world, the Church is like a great ship being pounded by the waves of life's different stresses. Our duty is not to abandon ship, but to keep her on her course.

Let us stand fast in what is right, and prepare our souls for trial. Let us wait upon God's strengthening and say to him: 'O Lord, you have been our refuge in all generations'.

9 June

St E

PHREM THE SYRIAN There was certainly hymn-singing in Christian churches before the time of St Ephrem – in the earliest Christian communities they sang psalms and there are other hymns which have left traces in the New Testament – but St Ephrem is the first writer of them to be definitely identifiable. He came from Nisibis, now called Nuseybin in south-east Turkey. It was very much a frontier town and, during Ephrem's time there, was besieged by the Persians three times. On the last occasion the Persian King dammed the river and flooded the outskirts of the city, an event to which Ephrem refers in one of his hymns; more than 400 of these have survived.

He was probably born about the year 306. He was baptized as an adult, but that was the common practice at the time, and it does not mean that his parents were pagans. On the contrary, it seems quite likely from what little evidence the saint gives in his writings that they were Christians. Their language was Syriac, a language related to the Aramaic Jesus spoke. From this Christian community came the richest literature of any in the Near East, and Ephrem's many writings – he produced commentaries on Scripture and polemics against some of the heretics of his day as well as composing hymns – are probably the most important. St Jerome, writing only nineteen years after Ephrem's death, says that the saint's writings were sometimes read out in church after the Scriptures. He had himself read some of them, he added, although in a Greek translation, and had been impressed by his high intelligence.

In 325 the Bishop of Nisibis was Jacob, also acknowledged as a saint, and it was he who went to the Council of Nicaea to join in the condemnation of Arius and to assert, against Arius, the divinity of Christ. When Jacob returned he appointed Ephrem to be a deacon of his church, and to teach catechism to those seeking baptism. A baptistery, built when Ephrem was working for the Bishop of Nisibis, still survives in Nuseybin.

The Roman Emperor Julian the Apostate led an attack into Persian territory in 363 and was killed. The Romans sued for peace, and as part of the peace treaty, handed the city of Nisibis over to the Persian King. Part of the agreement was that all Christians should leave. Ephrem certainly left. He went a hundred miles west to the city of Edessa, now Urfa, and spent there the last ten years of his life. While he was there a great famine affected the region, and Ephrem was responsible for gathering in the starving both from the city and from the surrounding countryside so that they could be fed, in so far as there was food, and nursed in their illnesses. That was a year before he died. His death occurred in 373: that much is certain, but the date is less sure. The best attested day is 9 June, on which his feast is now kept.

Some of his biographers have described him as a monk, but that could not be correct. The monastic life did not reach Nisibis or Edessa until the end of Ephrem's days. His own vocation was very different. He was almost certainly a member of a movement called 'children of the covenant' which could be made up of either married or unmarried men and women – though if they were married they agreed, as members of this group, to live celibate lives. It seems that they took vows, and very ascetical vows, when they were baptized. One historian writing about Ephrem said that he never looked at a woman's face after he had taken these vows, but that sounds highly unlikely. For one thing, he wrote hymns for women's choirs.

Central to the spiritual life of the children of the covenant was not only the desire to imitate Christ, but the belief that they were, individually, brides of Christ just as the Church is described by St Paul as the Bride of Christ. It was of course an image or symbol, but, as a poet, Ephrem thought and wrote through the means of such symbols to create a powerful picture of men and women's relation to God. As 'children of God' they were, potentially, divine beings, thought Ephrem, and through the incarnation we are lifted up to God. As he wrote in one hymn,

> Divinity flew down and descended
> to raise and draw up humanity.
> The Son has made beautiful the servant's deformity,
> and he has become a god, just as he desired.

17 June

St ALBERT CHMIELOWSKI Like the rest of us, Popes are entitled to have favourites among the saints, and surely Albert Chmielowski must rank high among those to whom Pope John Paul II is particularly devoted. Before a crowd of over a million, he beatified him in the Meadows of Cracow on 28 June 1983. Only half-a-dozen years later, on 12 November 1989, he proclaimed him a saint. But there was much more to the story than that. Before he became Pope, Karol Wojtyla was deeply interested in the theatre. As a young man he had considered being an actor. Later he wrote plays. One of these plays was *Our God's Brother* whose central character, the 'God's brother' of the title, is Albert Chmielowski.

Or rather, Adam Chmielowski, for that was his baptismal name. He was born in the south of Poland, at Igolomia, on 20 August 1845. His parents died when he was young, and he was brought up by relatives. When he was eleven they sent him away to school at St Petersburg. He went on to Warsaw, and finally studied agriculture in central Poland.

In January 1863 he joined the Polish uprising against the Russians. That September he was wounded in battle, and captured: his left leg was amputated. When released he travelled to Paris and eventually to Munich, where he enrolled to study painting in the Academy of Fine Arts. He proved to be an extremely gifted artist, as well as a perceptive critic. But he was also deeply devout. In 1880, a decade after he had exhibited his first paintings in Cracow, he joined the Society of Jesus.

He did not suit the Jesuits, or the Jesuits did not suit him. After only six months he had a nervous breakdown, and was obliged to leave. He went to the country to live with his brother, who managed a large estate. He still felt that God was calling him to some great mission. Now he became a Franciscan tertiary, preaching to the peasants in the fields and then, after his return to Cracow in 1884, to the poor of the city.

In Cracow he met the Carmelite friar Rafael Kalinowski, who had also taken part in the 1863 uprising, and who was also to be beatified, alongside Adam, in 1983. Under his inspiration Adam developed a deep devotion to St John of the Cross. He also decided once more to try his vocation as a religious. But this time it was different. Instead of joining an order, in August 1887 he simply took a new name – Albert – and dressed humbly in a rough habit of sackcloth. The following year he made his vows before the Bishop of Cracow, Cardinal Dunajewski – yet another hero of 1863. With these vows began the Albertine Congregation, Brothers dedicated to the relief of poverty and the care of the sick. Two years later he founded the Albertine Sisters for the same purpose. The two congregations opened houses throughout Poland for the poor and for the homeless. Their charity, as his, was offered in equal measure to believers and unbelievers, to Catholics and to the large Jewish population that then existed in the country.

He was remembered for his joy, for his serenity, and for the absolute abandonment of goods (even to the extent of destroying many of his own paintings) which he undertook to be more like, and nearer to, the poor whom he served. He died on Christmas Day 1916. Vast numbers of the people of Cracow, led by their mayor, came to his funeral, and so did Bishop Adam Sapieha, who later, as Cardinal Archbishop of Cracow, during the German occupation hid Karol Wojtyla in his house as the future Pope studied for the priesthood.

Because it is not possible to commemorate important saints on 25 December, St Albert's feast is celebrated on 17 June.

22 June

St P

AULINUS OF NOLA In the early centuries of Christianity it was not the general practice to baptize babies: most Christians were baptized when they were adults. This did not mean, of course, that they came from pagan families, or had a pagan education. Paulinus of Nola was born into a Christian family in Bordeaux, about the year 355, but was not baptized until 389 when he was in his mid-thirties. He was educated by the poet Ausonius, who was for a time tutor to the future Emperor Gratian at Trier, and was able to help some of his former pupils on the road to fame and fortune.

Not that Paulinus needed any help. His family was rich, with lands in Gaul (France) and Spain. In 378 he became a senator, and then governor of – probably – Campania, a region of Italy centred on Capua. Living in Campania, he was near the shrine of St Felix at Cimitile near Nola, which each year attracted a crowd of pilgrims on the anniversary of the saint's death. Gratian died in 383, and the new Emperor was a heretic who persecuted the orthodox magistrates in the Empire. Paulinus, though still technically not a Christian, lost his post, and made his way home to Bordeaux. It seems that he passed by way of Milan, where he met the Bishop, St Ambrose, and it was from Ambrose that he received his first formal preparation for baptism.

Between his return home and his final reception into the Church he was a gentleman of leisure. During this time he travelled to Spain, and there met and married his wife Teresia. After his baptism he went back to Spain with his wife, possibly to escape persecution by the Emperor, and in Spain Teresia gave birth to a son, who unhappily survived only a few days. Possibly it was the death of their son that decided Paulinus and Teresia to change the manner of their comfortable life, to give away all their very considerable wealth – an event which caused quite a scandal at the time though Ambrose and other notable Christians of the day such as Sts Augustine and Jerome very much approved – and live thereafter celibate lives. Paulinus' wholehearted conversion caused an enormous stir. The people of Barcelona, where he was living, demanded that the bishop make him a priest even though he was not yet a deacon, and he was ordained in 394.

He was not content in Spain, and wanted to go back to Nola, and in particular to the shrine of St Felix, to whom he had dedicated himself when he was governor of Campania. He returned there in 395, built a church, a guest-house for pilgrims and an aqueduct, and created a community of like-minded holy men and women who lived a monastic-style existence on the upper floor of his home, while the ground floor was given over to guests, to the poor and to debtors. From Nola he wrote letters to the Christian leaders of his day who were his friends, such as Augustine, Jerome, Delphinus, the Bishop of Bordeaux who had baptized him, and to several others. He also wrote poems, from which a great deal can be learned about the world in which he lived. Before his baptism his poetry had been about worldly topics; after his baptism it was on Christian themes. And every year he wrote a poem in honour of St Felix.

Teresia, who seems to have looked after his semi-monastic community, died in 409. It was probably that same year that Paulinus was chosen as Bishop of Nola. Little is known about his pastoral work as a bishop, except that he wrote to St Augustine to ask him for a copy of his work on *The Care of the Dead*, and asked the Scripture scholar St Jerome for advice on difficult passages in the Bible. What remains are his letters and his poetry. They reveal a man who was much loved and admired by his many friends. Though he could be severe, as he was with Ausonius when he complained that

Paulinus was only writing poems about holy things, he was usually a very mild, kind and gentle man in his correspondence. Not all of his letters have survived – he wrote so many, he admitted, that he did not always recognize his own when he saw them – and through them built up a network of Christian friendship. With his friends, and from the quiet of his monastic retreat, he meditated in his letters on the teachings of scripture.

He died on 22 June 431. He had just celebrated the eucharist with two visiting bishops and had given money to the poor. It was the hour of vespers. He was buried at Nola, near the tomb of St Felix. His body was moved to Rome in the eleventh century, but taken back in 1909 on the instructions of Pope Pius X.

St Paulinus wrote:

An athlete has not won when he has laid aside his clothing: it is then that the contest begins and on its issue hangs the crown.

St

ANTHONY MARY ZACCARIA
The first half of the sixteenth century throughout Europe was a time of terrible devastation by war. It was also a period when the spiritual life of the Church was perhaps at its lowest ebb. But even at that low point there emerged a number of holy men and women who sought to revitalize the Church from within, often by the reformation of existing religious orders, or by the formation of new ones. Anthony Mary Zaccaria falls into the second group.

He was born in Cremona in 1502. His father Lazzaro died when he was only a few months old. He was brought up by his mother Antonietta as a devout and compassionate child, and when he was eighteen he decided to go to the University of Padua to study medicine. At the University he spent four years, and returned home in 1524.

But once back in his home town he gave his attention to teaching the catechism, at least as much as to being a doctor. His spiritual director was a Dominican, and this friar suggested to him that, so great was his devotion, he might consider becoming a priest. He studied theology, and was ordained in 1528: at his first mass he saw a vision of angels standing about the altar.

As a priest he enjoyed at Cremona the wealthy benefice of the church of St George. He worked hard trying to form groups of lay people who could themselves serve as a leaven to the rest of society. To give himself more time for this labour he resigned the benefice and became chaplain to Louisa Torelli, Countess of Guastalla, and, in 1539, moved with her to Milan.

There he joined the Confraternity of Holy Wisdom, an association mainly of lay people who were dedicated to improving their own spiritual lives. He rapidly became the leading person in the Confraternity. He so imbued some of its members with his own desire for reform of Christian life that there grew out of it three new congregations within the Church. All of them were named after St Paul, to whom Anthony Mary had a particular devotion.

One of these was under the direction of Countess Guastalla, and was called 'the Angelicals of St Paul'. It was the earliest congregation of women who were not strictly enclosed nuns, and who were devoted to a direct apostolate: its members were chiefly concerned with the pastoral care of women and young girls. A second, consisting of married people, assisted the 'Angelicals' and the priests associated with Anthony Mary.

This organization of priests, originally known simply as 'the Sons of St Paul' and later as the Clerks Regular of St Paul, was the first of the three societies to be approved by the Pope. Its members rapidly became known as 'Barnabites', for the first church to be entrusted to their care was that of St Barnabas, in Milan.

In order to shock the populace of Milan into a more Christian way of life, Anthony Mary asked the Barnabites and the Angelicals to process through the streets of the city carrying out stern penitential practices. As far as the people of Milan were concerned such dramatic sights were successful in spurring them to a holier way of life, but many of the other priests of the city thought differently. They denounced Anthony Mary to the authorities in Rome, and he was twice put on trial – and twice totally exonerated.

The result of these tribunals was the opposite of what Anthony Mary's adversaries had intended: they left him and his congregation immeasurably strengthened in their work of reform. They continued preaching in the churches and on the streets of Milan. Anthony Mary had a deep devotion to the eucharist and, although the early history of the practice of the Forty Hours adoration before the Blessed Sacrament is unclear, it seems likely that it was he who made it a ceremony open to the public, if he did not himself invent it. He encouraged frequent, even daily, communion, a thing then unheard of. He also began the practice of ringing a bell at three o'clock every Friday afternoon as a reminder to those who might hear it of Jesus' death upon the cross.

He served as superior of the Clerks Regular for only three years. He resigned the office in favour of one of his first followers, and went off to Vicenza, to begin his missionary work all over again. But he did not have long to live. While attempting to resolve an ecclesiastical squabble in Guastalla he was taken ill, worn out by both the hard work and the severe mortification to which he constantly submitted his body.

As he lay dying he was taken back to Cremona, to his mother's house. There he died, on 5 July 1539, when he was little more than thirty-seven years old. He was buried first in the church of St Paul, in Milan, but in 1891 his remains were transferred to the church of St Barnabas. In 1897, on 27 May, he was formally declared a saint.

13 July

LELIA BARBIERI To found a religious order is usually the work of a lifetime. So it was, indeed, with Clelia Barbieri – except that her life was so short that she bears the title of the youngest person in the history of the Church to have founded one.

She was born on 13 February 1847 in a village not far from Bologna in Italy. Her mother Giacinta Nannetti came from rich parents: her father Giuseppe was a labourer who worked for Giacinta's uncle, the local doctor. Giacinta was deeply devout, and she brought up her daughter – who had been christened Clelia Rachele Maria – as equally so. When Clelia was only eight years old her father died in a cholera epidemic. Giacinta's uncle, the doctor, provided better accommodation for the family (there was also a younger daughter, Ernestina), but they still had to struggle to earn a living by taking in sewing, and by spinning and weaving the coarse woollen material typical of the region.

Clelia's piety was exemplary. If she was not at home working, it was common to find her in church praying, and she was allowed to make her first communion at a (then) unusually early age of eleven. On that day – 17 June 1858 – she had her first mystical experience, a deep sense of her own sinfulness, together with a feeling of contrition for her own failings and for those of the whole world.

That experience set the pattern for the rest of her short life. She was frequently rapt in her own private prayer and meditation. But she was also deeply committed to the help of her neighbours, of the poor and of those untutored in the faith. She herself had been slow to learn to read: after she had done so she began to teach catechism to the girls with whom she worked. There was at that time an organization of catechists in the district called 'Workers for Christian Catechism'.

When Clelia wanted to join it she was at first rebuffed, but later admitted as an assistant teacher. Her success was such, however, that soon she became a leader of the local group.

Clelia was renowned for her beauty. Though she had many offers of marriage she was convinced that God was calling her to another form of life. Her skill and her unshakeable faith drew other young women to her catechists' group. With the encouragement of their local parish priest and Clelia's spiritual adviser, the small band decided to form themselves into a congregation. Clelia was the unquestioned leader.

The idea had first arisen when Clelia was not yet twenty, but such was the unrest in Italy that it was not until May 1868 that she and three companions could move into the house where once they had met as 'Workers for Christian Catechism'. They called their congregation the Little Sisters of Our Lady of Sorrows, and put themselves under the patronage of St Francesco di Paola: Our Lady of Sorrows was a particular devotion in that region of Italy, and Francesco di Paola was the patron saint of the village church.

As a religious community they continued Clelia's work, instructing children in the catechism, looking after the poor and the sick, and in general assisting the priest in his pastoral care of the parish. But to this they added at Clelia's insistence a period of prayer and meditation, so that the community brought together both action and contemplation.

The first years of the community were a constant struggle to survive, frequently succeeding only because of what they took to be the intervention of divine providence. Their devotion, like that of their founder, centred on the Passion of Christ, upon which Clelia herself constantly meditated.

Clelia had long suffered from tuberculosis. Two years after the foundation of the Little Sisters of Our Lady of Sorrows the infection flared up. She died on 13 July 1870, when she was only twenty-three years of age. A year after her death, when the community she had founded was at prayer, all those present heard her voice speaking to them. Clelia was beatified by Pope Paul VI in 1968, and canonized by Pope John Paul II on 9 April 1989.

14 July

St

FRANCIS SOLANO In 1726 two men were declared saints who had lived in the same city of the New World at the same time: St Turibius de Mongrevejo and St Francis Solano. The first was Archbishop of Lima, the second a humble Franciscan friar with a marvellous ability for bringing people closer to God. They were not the first saints of the Americas. That title belongs to St Rose, who was also then living in Lima. She, however, had been born there: both Turibius and Francis came from Spain.

Francis Solano came from a family of minor nobility which was comfortably provided for, if not exactly wealthy. His family lived at Montilla in Andalusia, and he was born there, Matteo and Anna's second child, on 10 March 1549. Though schooled by the Jesuits, at the age of twenty he decided to join the Observant Franciscans and was sent to Seville for his studies. He was ordained there in 1576. He was always rigorously careful in keeping the rule, and within five years of his ordination he was appointed by his superiors to be master of novices. When bubonic plague broke out in a town near the novitiate he was unstinting in the service of those affected. He even caught the plague himself, but managed to recover.

His generous dedication to the poor, the sick and the imprisoned, and perhaps more particularly his remarkable skill as a preacher, brought him the veneration of the people of Andalusia. To escape this unwanted fame he begged to be allowed to go as a missionary to Africa. But the King of Spain needed priests in his new territories; so he was sent to South America, and his adventures began.

He and another eleven friars arrived in Cartagena in May 1589. They then travelled on foot across the isthmus of Panama and there took ship again for Peru. There were some eighty African slaves aboard, and Francis made himself their chaplain. When the ship struck a sandbank and the crew took to the lifeboats, Francis stayed with the abandoned slaves in the stranded hull of their ship for three days. After the storm had abated they were rescued and Francis continued his way to Lima.

When he arrived there, however, he was told that his apostolate lay in Tucumán, some three thousand kilometres to the south-west, across the Andes in the northern part of what is now Argentina. He set off again and for the next four and a half years laboured among the Indian population in Tucumán. He learned their dialects: it was said his preaching led to the baptism of 200,000 people of that region.

To all he worked among – first the slaves, then the native peoples, then those of Spanish descent or of mixed race – he was a devoted pastor and an extraordinarily powerful preacher. In December 1604 he went about the streets and squares of Lima proclaiming, as Jonah was required to proclaim in Nineveh, that the wrath of God would fall upon the city and destroy it if its citizens did not reform their lives. So vivid was his picture of the destruction that would ensue that the people panicked, almost rioted. The Viceroy was alarmed, and consulted the archbishop. Turibius asked Francis to return to the streets to explain that he was proclaiming the destruction of souls rather than the collapse of buildings. The population calmed down.

Despite all this, Francis Solano was no wild-eyed prophet of doom. He was strict with himself especially in observance of the rule, but he was essentially a cheerful, friendly man, never happier than when he was playing his lute for the entertainment of his Franciscan brothers – and before the statue of the Virgin Mary.

In 1608 he was taken ill in Lima, and died there, two years later, on 14 July, the feast of that other great Franciscan St

Bonaventure. He is greatly honoured in Lima and in southern Spain, and is especially invoked for help in times of drought.

A saying of St Francis Solano

> My object was to reconcile, and having succeeded in it
> I have suffered nothing.

31 July

St I

GNATIUS LOYOLA There are some saints, their names safely recorded in medieval legend and handed down to us, who never existed – Christopher, Barbara, Catherine of Alexandria for example. Then there are saints who undoubtedly existed yet around whom legends so quickly grew up that they almost obscure the saint's true character. It is perhaps true of St Francis of Assisi; it is certainly true of St Ignatius Loyola, the founder of the Society of Jesus, the Jesuits.

According to the myth, Ignatius was a soldier-saint, his followers trained in a military mould. But Ignatius was not a soldier. If he had a career before his conversion it was as a diplomat. He carried a sword – and had used it – but then that was true of all the nobility of early sixteenth-century Spain. He took part in only one major battle, defending the city of Pamplona from the French. The defenders were outnumbered, and knew it. The professional soldiers wanted to surrender, but Ignatius (who was there more or less by accident), inflamed by thoughts of honour and glory, insisted they fight on. He was wounded in the leg by a cannon ball, and the city surrendered anyway. The French sent him home on a stretcher.

Home was the castle of Loyola, in north-eastern Spain, near the French border. He had been born there, almost certainly in 1491 though the exact date is unknown, and was baptized Iñigo. When he was about 15 he was sent to the court of Ferdinand and Isabella, and lived in the household of the high treasurer. 'He was particularly careless about gambling, affairs with women, and the use of arms', wrote his secretary many years later. He had a brush with the law, but claimed the exemption of the Church because he was – technically – a cleric.

There was very little to read at Loyola as he recovered from his wound. He had to make do with the lives of the saints and with Ludolph the Carthusian's *Life of Christ*. Their impact was profound, especially that of Ludolph (Iñigo considered becoming a Carthusian himself). He went on pilgrimage to the black Madonna of Montserrat, near Barcelona, and settled down for nearly a year beneath the mountain of Montserrat, to live a hermit's life in a cave beside the river Cardoner.

It was a time of prayer, of meditation, of fasting (perhaps a little too much fasting) and penance. He saw visions, and was illumined by God. He read the *Imitation of Christ*, and afterwards said he never wanted to read any other book of devotion. He wrote the *Spiritual Exercises*, which remain the best guide to his piety, and to understanding the spirituality of the Jesuits. The *Exercises* are built around Christ's life: the events are to be imagined, and then meditated upon in all their detail of what was said, of the people present, of the locations in which they took place. Ignatius went off to Jerusalem to view the sites of Jesus' death, resurrection and ascension. He wanted to stay, but the Franciscans who guarded the holy places would not let him.

Back in Spain he decided that, if he were to help souls find God, he had better be educated. When he was preaching in Spain he fell under the eye of the Inquisition, and twice ended up in prison. He went to France, to the University in Paris, and in March 1535 he became a Master of Arts. He was now licensed to teach.

But he was also the leader of a small group of men who were destined to become the first Jesuits. They took vows together in a small chapel on Montmartre on 15 August 1534. They were to live in poverty, devote themselves to the salvation of others, make a pilgrimage to Jerusalem if possible and, if not, to put themselves under the command of the Pope. It proved impossible to get to Jerusalem and the companions, who had scattered, met up again in Venice in 1537 where, in June that year, seven of them were ordained. Then they left for Rome.

On the way, at a wayside shrine called La Storta nine miles from Rome, Ignatius had a mystical experience, a vision of the Trinity in which God the Father said to him: 'I will be favourable to you in Rome.' This confirmed him in his vocation, and in his desire to found the Society. The Society was formally approved in 1540, and the following year Ignatius was elected its first superior. Then, for the next fifteen years, Ignatius sat at a desk, writing letters, negotiating, offering spiritual counsel, but most of all drawing up a constitution which enshrined his spirit so that subsequent generations of Jesuits would understand what he had perceived the call of Christ to be. He had wanted to save souls, but the missionary journeys he had to leave to others, and especially to Francis Xavier, one of his first companions.

Ignatius Loyola died suddenly, without the comfort of the sacraments, on 31 July 1556. He was canonized in 1622, at the same time as Francis Xavier.

A prayer of St Ignatius Loyola

Teach us, good Lord, to serve thee as thou deservest;
to give, and not to count the cost,
to fight, and not to heed the wounds,
to toil, and not to seek for rest,
to labour, and not to ask for any reward,
save that of knowing that we do thy will.

1 August

St

ALPHONSUS DE' LIGUORI There are many unusual conversion stories in the lives of the saints but perhaps few as strange as that of Alphonsus. He was born in the Kingdom of Naples in 1696: his father was the commander of the royal galleys. He was early destined for a brilliant career as a lawyer, passing final examinations as a doctor in both laws, civil and canon, when only sixteen. He went on to practise law. He was no more than ordinarily devout, but, in the Lent of 1723, after pondering for a year on the retreat he had made twelve months earlier, he came to the conclusion that he would not marry. Yet he still had not made up his mind to be ordained.

Then he lost a case. It is sometimes claimed that it was the only one he ever did lose. Be that as it may, the fact devastated him. It was all the worse because he seems to have lost through carelessness. He immediately gave up the law, and tried to become a priest of the Oratory. His father endeavoured to dissuade him. Alphonsus went along with his father to the extent of agreeing not to become an Oratorian, but to study, and live, at home: in 1726 he was ordained.

He had been a lawyer, a profession which relied on speech-making. He now preached highly successfully up and down the Kingdom of Naples. He became friendly with a priest, Thomas Falcoia, who was trying to establish a religious order. Falcoia was appointed Bishop of Castellamare, and he invited Alphonsus to join him. The bishop now suggested that Alphonsus should start a congregation of priest-missionaries, to work among the peasants of the Italian countryside. On 9 November 1732, in Scala near Amalfi, the Congregation of the Most Holy Redeemer, the Redemptorists, came into being with Bishop Falcoia as its superior. It did not work. There was dissension among the new members, some opting

91

for Falcoia and others, a very few, for Alphonsus. The saint was eventually left with only a single recruit but then others came, and in 1734 a second foundation had to be made. Alphonsus could go back to his preaching supported by members of his congregation who, after the death of the bishop in 1743, finally took vows and drew up a constitution.

The Redemptorists were now attacked for being Jesuits under another name – the Society of Jesus having recently been suppressed – and Alphonsus decided to get royal approval for his foundation. He was deceived by a priest at court who altered the Redemptorist Rule, unbeknown to Alphonsus, stripping its members of vows so they were technically no longer religious. Alphonsus, old by this time, and crippled with arthritis, signed the document without properly reading it.

The King of Naples insisted that the Redemptorists in his dominion keep to the new rule: the Pope demanded that, in the papal states, the old rule be retained. The Pope also insisted that only members who lived by the original version were true Redemptorists, and appointed a new superior, thereby excluding Alphonsus from the order he had founded. The two branches were not reunited until after his death.

Despite all these struggles he found time to write – especially the great works on moral theology for which he has been given the title of Doctor of the Church. He also wrote a book, *The Glories of Mary*, which seems to bestow on the Blessed Virgin almost divine attributes. Mary was only one aspect of his devotional life. In all his struggles over the young congregation, and in all the sufferings ill-health brought him in the second half of his life, he was sustained above all by devotion to the eucharist and by the conviction that, wherever he might be, he was in the presence of God. He was dedicated to restoring the practice of the faith in the Italian countryside, especially when, from 1762 to 1775, he served as Bishop of Sant' Agata dei Goti.

In the final months he was particularly attacked by the scruples which had plagued him on and off all his life. But these dark hours were often broken by ecstasies and by miracles. His death, on 1 August 1787, was a peaceful one.

14 August

St M

AXIMILIAN KOLBE In June 1979, during his first journey as Pope to his native Poland, John Paul II made a detour to Auschwitz. There, in the concentration camp where so many thousands of Jews and others had died, he laid flowers, and knelt, on the concrete floor of the death cell of Maximilian Kolbe. The camp lay within the borders of the diocese the Pope, as Archbishop of Cracow, had governed. Just over three years later, on 10 October 1982, John Paul II declared him a saint. He is remembered chiefly for the manner of his death, yet his life of dedicated devotion to the Virgin Mary was no less remarkable.

He was born at ZdunskaWola on 7 January 1894 and baptized Raymond: the name Maximilian was given to him when he became a Franciscan. He had studied with the Franciscan Conventuals, as did his two brothers, then joined the order, taking his first vows in September 1911. He went to Rome, studying philosophy under the Jesuits, and theology with the Franciscans. On 28 April 1918 he was ordained, and in 1919 he returned to Poland.

His life's work had already begun. At the age of ten he received what he believed to be a vision of Mary, holding out to him two crowns, one white, one red. While in Rome, in October 1917, he decided to start a 'Militia of Mary Immaculate', a worldwide association dedicated to devotion to Our Lady. His return to Poland was marked by ill-health. The Militia seemed to founder. But on his recovery he began anew, establishing a large number of groups organized along 'professional' lines – so that there was, for example, a group for the Franciscans who had supported him from the beginning, another for college students, and so on. To link them he began a periodical, *The Knight of the Immaculate*, which he printed in great numbers and largely gave away as another means of recruitment. By the end of the 1920s membership was nearly a quarter of a million in Poland alone.

The saint's next venture was to start a special friary dedicated to Our Lady. He was given land just west of Warsaw, and built huts on it for his Franciscan followers. He called it Niepokalanow, or 'Mary's City'. By the end of 1929 there were well over a hundred Franciscans in residence, at different stages of their training. By the outbreak of war, just a decade later, there were over eight hundred friars attached to it, producing eleven different publications – including a daily newspaper. *The Knight* alone printed a million copies.

Despite this phenomenal success, Maximilian was unsatisfied. In 1930 he determined to take his campaign of arousing devotion to the Mother of God to the Far East. China was his chosen territory, but the hierarchy would not have him. He went on to Japan. The Bishop of Nagasaki was unenthusiastic – until he discovered that Kolbe had two doctorates. He asked him to stay and teach in the seminary. Kolbe stayed: but immediately set in hand the publication in Japanese of *The Knight*. The first edition appeared only a month after his arrival.

The first little group of Franciscans who arrived in Japan with Kolbe met some resistance – including from Canadian Franciscans – but they finally flourished, adding new Japanese recruits to their number. Kolbe moved on to India to establish further 'cities of Mary' but, in 1936, he was called back to Poland to head the original Niepokalanow.

Shortly after the fall of Poland Kolbe was briefly imprisoned, only to be rearrested on 17 February 1941. He spent some time in prison in Warsaw and then, on 28 May, was sent to Auschwitz. It was the German practice, should anyone escape from Auschwitz, to sentence ten prisoners to death. When, at the end of July, men from the block in which Kolbe lived were paraded to be selected for death because of an escape, he offered himself, as an old man, he said, with no dependants, in place of an army sergeant, Francis Gajowniczek, who had a wife and children.

Maximilian Kolbe was condemned to the bunker with his nine fellows. They were starved for two weeks, though for as long as they survived the saint tried to keep up their spirits with hymns and prayers. At the end of the time just four were left alive. Kolbe, with the others, was given a lethal injection. He died on the vigil of the Assumption, 14 August 1941. He had always hoped, he had told friends, that he would die on a feast of the Mother of God.

25 August

St LOUIS IX OF FRANCE The names of members of the royal families of medieval Europe are regularly to be found listed in the calendar of the saints of the Church. That is not surprising: they were prominent people. Any sign of holiness of life was likely to be seized upon by their subjects, and the ruler (or ruler's consort) then made the subject of veneration after his or her death. No series of lives of saints, therefore, should be without the story of at least one king or queen, and few are more deserving of mention than King Louis IX of France.

He was born in Poissy on 25 April 1215 and, because he received there the grace of baptism, he always signed himself in later life as 'Louis of Poissy'. His father was Louis VIII (not yet King when Louis of Poissy was born) and his mother was Blanche of Castile, whose own mother was Eleanor of England. So Louis IX had an English grandmother and, when he married Margaret of Provence in 1234, he gained King Henry III of England as a brother-in-law. Louis IX succeeded to the throne on 7 November 1226, when only eleven years old: Blanche became regent, and ensured that her son was not overthrown by having him crowned almost immediately.

It was an era in France of great achievement. The splendid gothic cathedrals were being built; the Sorbonne was founded; St Thomas Aquinas taught in Paris during Louis' lifetime. Louis was renowned for ruling France with justice and with some success in regaining the territory of his country from the English. In December 1244 he was taken very seriously ill, and believed that he was healed by a piece of the True Cross which the Latin Emperor of Constantinople had sent to him, out of that city's rich store of relics. On his recovery he announced his intention of going on a crusade to recover the Holy Land for Christianity.

The expedition sailed four years later (the King having raised part of the money by taxing the Church). He was at first successful in battle, though he was unable to control the violence of his troops as they plundered the city of Damietta in Egypt. But then disease struck the crusading army, and in 1250 Louis was defeated and taken prisoner. He negotiated his own release, and that of his troops who had survived – the wounded and sick had been slaughtered after the defeat – and sailed on to the Holy Land. He visited such of the Holy Places he could, helped the Christians in Syria, and returned home in 1254 upon hearing of the death of Blanche, whom he had left in charge of France. He again went on the crusade in 1270, this time landing near Tunis because he had heard – wrongly, as it turned out – that the Emir might convert to Christianity. Shortly after landing he was taken ill. Almost the last thing he did before he died on 24 August 1270 was to urge the Greek ambassadors who were in his camp to reunite their Church with the Church of Rome.

Louis was canonized in 1297, but long before that he was being called a saint and 'the most Christian king'. It was a title he was given for his holiness of life, rather than for his relatively unsuccessful exploits as a crusader. One of the most admired traits of his character was his generosity. He gave away vast sums of money to the poor, and to religious causes of all kinds. He was such a supporter of the Dominicans and Franciscans that he was included in the list of saints proper to each of them. But he also gave money to other religious groups, and particularly to the Beguines, women who lived a form of communal life but without vows, and worked among the poor and the sick. The king himself had an especial concern for the sick, and endowed hospitals in Paris and elsewhere, as well as giving money to individuals who were ill, such as lepers.

The King had an enormous devotion to the relics of saints but his greatest veneration was for the relics of Christ's passion. They were acquired from the Emperor of Constantinople, and Sainte-Chapelle in Paris was built by Louis to house them – the relics of the Crown of Thorns in particular. He was also a peacemaker. He negotiated with Henry III a peace that was more generous to the English King than his lack of success on the battlefield might have led him to expect. He made peace with other neighbouring powers, and so great was his reputation that rulers came to seek his assistance as an arbiter. Not all his counsellors understood his efforts to prevent Christian fighting Christian; not all his efforts at arbitration were successful; but Louis was a King who stood by what, in the middle years of the thirteenth century, he took to be the moral obligations of a Christian ruler.

St Louis' advice

Be careful not knowingly to do or say anything which, were all the world to know it, you could not gladly admit and say 'Yes, I did that', or 'I said it'.

St

ARGARET WARD Three of the Forty Martyrs of England and Wales, canonized together by Pope Paul VI on 25 October 1970, were women: Margaret Clitherow, Margaret Ward and Anne Line. They were, in order, the wife of a butcher, a servant, and a priest's housekeeper. Though there is a full account of Margaret Clitherow, written by one of the priests to whom she gave shelter in York, little is known of the other two, and especially of Margaret Ward. Yet enough has survived to demonstrate that she was a person of spirit, courage and resourcefulness far beyond the ordinary.

Margaret Ward came from Congleton in Cheshire. Her parents might now be called middle-class, but certainly not rich. Her date of birth is unknown, though it must have been somewhere in the middle of the sixteenth century. She entered into the service of a Mrs Whittel, who lived in London.

Perhaps Mrs Whittel was a Catholic: Margaret certainly was. When she heard that a priest, William Watson, was imprisoned in the Bridewell and in a very bad state, she determined to visit him.

Her ministrations to Fr Watson brought about her execution. He was himself eventually put to death (in November 1603), but he has not been included in the lists of the martyrs. He turned out not to be a particularly pleasant character: 'Apart from his agility at getting out of prisons', a biographer has written about him, 'he had few attractive characteristics... he was a great eccentric if not actually mad.'

Margaret Ward knew none of this. All she saw was a priest in gaol needing help. She willingly gave it. She took a basket of food and, when entrance to the prison was denied her, made friends with the gaoler's wife. Even so her visits were treated with suspicion. For a month, as she came into the Bridewell, the pies or the loaves in her basket were each broken open to ensure that nothing was concealed within them.

It seems that Watson himself suggested he might escape if only she could bring him a long enough rope. When the warders were off their guard and no longer searching her basket, she brought one in, apparently hidden beneath a clean shirt. She also arranged that a boatman should meet Fr Watson after his escape to carry him away down river, but at the last minute the man she had employed refused to help. By chance she met an Irishman, John Roche, whom she knew slightly and to whom she told her story. He took over. Unhappily for John Roche and Margaret Ward, the escape did not go according to plan. As he clambered down the wall by the rope, either Fr Watson dislodged a stone which created enough noise to rouse the warders, or he simply fell. Either way, he and Roche were chased through Lambeth Marsh, where Roche exchanged clothes with the priest to aid his escape. Roche himself, however, was captured.

And so, the following morning, was Margaret Ward. The gaoler, when shown the rope Fr Watson had used, said it could only have been brought in by her. She was promptly arrested and so badly tortured that she was crippled. A few days later she was brought to court. It is known that the trial took place on 26 August, and that Margaret had been in prison for eight days before that; so it looks as if the escape took place on 18 August 1588, but the date is uncertain.

When questioned in court, Margaret denied she had committed any offence against Queen Elizabeth. She had done no more, she said charitably, than the Queen herself would have done in similar circumstances. She was offered her freedom if she would consent to attend the Protestant church. She flatly refused, and was condemned: John Roche was also condemned to die. Along with three other lay people and a

priest, she and John Roche suffered martyrdom at Tyburn on
30 August. The small group sang all the way along the road
to their execution.

St P

ETER CLAVER Peter Claver died on 8 September 1654. By the rule which determines a saint's feast – the day of his or her 'birthday into heaven' – he should be fêted on the same day as the birthday of Our Lady. But he is not. His celebration occurs a day later, on 9 September. That his feast should be moved so that it is not overshadowed by the Nativity of Our Lady is a sign of how much he is revered, especially perhaps in the Americas in general and in the United States in particular.

He was born in Verdu, Catalonia, about the year 1580. He went to study at the university in Barcelona in preparation for the priesthood, but instead of committing himself to a distinguished career in the Church – and his acuteness of mind signalled that he might rise high – he chose instead to join the Society of Jesus. He was sent to the Jesuit College at Palma in Majorca where he met Alphonsus Rodriguez, a lay brother whose reputation for sanctity far outshone his humble role of keeper of the door. Perhaps one future saint recognized another: Peter Claver and Alphonsus became firm friends, and Alphonsus encouraged Peter to volunteer to work on the Jesuit missions. And to the missions he went, though not until 1610 and after further theological studies. He went to what was is now Colombia, and to the city of Cartagena, one of the principal centres of the slave trade. He was ordained priest in Cartagena in 1615.

For his dedication, Peter Claver has been called the saint of the slave trade. It is a title he earned over and over again by his ministrations not only to the souls but also to the bodies of the men and women who had been brought to Cartagena in the most degrading conditions, penned in worse than cattle, many dying of starvation, thirst, or of simple overcrowding on the long journey from the west coast of Africa. Peter was not the first Jesuit to engage in this apostolic work. He joined a group organized by another member of the Society, Alfonso de Sandoval.

Though the slave traffickers were willing to placate the Church by allowing their human cargoes to be baptized, they had no interest in doing anything else. Peter instructed slaves in the faith, sometimes with the help of an interpreter, more often, perhaps, by sign language and holy pictures. It seemed to work. In his forty years' apostolate he is estimated to have baptized well over a quarter of a million people. The white slave-owners complained to him and to his superiors. They said he was wasting the slaves' valuable time. He was turning them to singing hymns and to praying, they said indignantly, instead of to working.

It was not only slaves who received his care. He ministered to the sick, whether black or white, in Cartagena's two hospitals. He was much in demand, in those violent times, as a chaplain to those about to die, many of whom he succeeded in reconciling to God before their execution. He went out to preach retreats, sometimes into the countryside where he would refuse to stay with the wealthy landowners, preferring instead the simple dwelling of a slave.

When the plague struck Cartagena in 1650 Peter Claver was preaching to black congregations up the coast. He fell victim to the illness, and had to be brought back to Cartagena. He was bedridden for a long time, occasionally being carried on a stretcher to visit some friend, or to a condemned prisoner, or to the hospital. The plague took the lives of a number of the Jesuits, and many of those whom it spared gave their time to helping the sick. The other sick, that is, for now that Peter could no longer go about his business his brothers in the Society appear to have neglected him.

On 6 September he felt the approach of death, and by the evening had gone into a coma. Thousands came to visit him in his cell – and to steal a relic of someone they all, black or white, knew to be a saint – though he was not canonized until 1888. After his death, the city authorities buried him in great style, and at public expense. Indians and blacks had a celebration of their own, to which they invited their masters.

17 September

St **H**ILDEGARD OF BINGEN Some saints receive great devotion for a period of time and then, if they are not entirely forgotten, the interest of Christians shifts to other models of holiness seemingly more in keeping with the needs of the time. But just occasionally the veneration of a particular holy man or woman undergoes a revival. And of no one can this be more true that of St Hildegard of Bingen. For some eight centuries she had been more or less forgotten, her vast range of writings unread. But in the last twenty years there has been greatly renewed interest in, and devotion to, this most astounding mystic and church leader.

She was born in 1098 in Germany: the village was called Bermersheim. Her family was wealthy, members of the minor nobility, and when, at the age of eight, she was put into a Benedictine monastery, she was placed in the charge of Jutta, a young noblewoman, and the daughter of a family known to Hildegard's.

Her religious life began as an anchorite, that is to say, she was walled up with Jutta and some servants in a small suite of rooms beside the abbey church of Disibodenberg. Eventually, however, they adopted the formal rule of the Benedictines and, at the age of fifteen, Hildegard became a nun. In 1136 Jutta died, and Hildegard was elected to lead the community.

All this time she had been having visions – she reported later that she had been having them ever since she had been in her mother's womb. She had not told anyone about them apart from Jutta, and Jutta had told the monk Volmar, who, under the abbot of Disibodenberg, was in charge of the nuns. In 1141 God told her to make the visions known. She confided in Volmar, and Volmar asked her to record them.

That is how she came to write the *Scivias*, a remarkable Latin text representing truths of the faith in visionary form.

It won her fame – but she was still nervous about putting her experiences into words. She asked, and won, the support of St Bernard of Clairvaux for these accounts of her inner experiences, and a couple of years later the approval of Pope Eugenius III. She gained in confidence.

Hildegard was, however, unhappy that men should be in charge of communities of women and she longed for a monastery of her own. The monks of Disibodenberg opposed her leaving – but she went anyway, taking her community down the river Nahe to Rupertsberg. In considerable difficulties, not least from shortage of funds, she founded a house which won its independence. Not that she was a revolutionary: only those of noble birth were allowed to join her convent. Meanwhile she went on writing – a book on the world about her, another on medicine, a third, again of visionary experiences, which reflected her problems in the new monastery.

She was now famous. She determined to build upon her fame by preaching in the surrounding countryside, something unheard of for a cloistered abbess of some sixty years. But for twelve years she did so, while writing yet another great visionary work, a study of God's operation in Creation which has made her something of a patron saint to those Christians actively engaged with ecological concerns.

She was a woman who loved much – perhaps a little too much sometimes, for it seems she could be overbearing. She was devoted to the life of prayer in the cloister, but met, and exchanged letters with, the Emperor Frederick Barbarossa (she even told him he was acting childishly, and would be cut off from God's grace if he did not repent). She was frequently ill, her major bouts of illness coinciding with major changes in her life. She advised people to behave with discretion, though she scarcely did so herself. Her regime was strict, but she could be sympathetic to human frailty. She designed a new, rather flamboyant, habit for her nuns. Above all she composed music for them to sing, based partly on the traditional plainchant and partly on inspiration from her visions.

She died on 17 September 1179. Moves for her canonization soon began, but it never happened. In the fifteenth century, however, her name was placed in the Roman Martyrology, the official list of saints, and her feast, on 17 September, is celebrated throughout Germany.

Part of a hymn to Mary by Hildegard

Now let the whole Church
Sing with joy and
Resound with music
For the sweetest Virgin,
Mary, most worthy of praise,
Mother of God. Amen.

19 September

St **T**HEODORE When St Bede was composing *The History of the English Church and People* in his monastery at Jarrow in the second decade of the eighth century, he looked back upon the time when Theodore governed the Church at Canterbury as a golden age. 'Never had there been such happy times as these since the English settled in Britain', he wrote. 'The people eagerly sought the new-found joys of the kingdom of heaven, and all who wished for instruction in reading the Scriptures found teachers ready to hand.'

Almost everything we know about Theodore comes from Bede. Strangely, until the eleventh century no one bothered to write his biography. But there are many routes to holiness, and that taken by Theodore was one of selfless scholarship and utter devotion to fostering the organizational, as well as the spiritual, life of Christianity in England. He was, says Bede, 'the first archbishop whom the entire English Church obeyed'.

He was born at Tarsus in Cilicia, the birthplace of the Apostle Paul, at the very beginning of the seventh century. He was educated in Athens, but by 666 was living in Italy. That was the year that the Archbishop-elect of Canterbury died in Rome, where he had gone to receive papal approval. After much searching, the Pope chose Theodore as a substitute. Theodore was not yet even a subdeacon. At the age of sixty-five he was swiftly propelled through the ranks of the priesthood and consecrated bishop. On 27 May 669 he arrived to take possession of his cathedral, exactly a year after leaving Rome. For someone quite old Theodore displayed a quite extraordinary vigour in administering the English Church. The division between the two distinct forms of churchmanship, Roman and Celtic, had been resolved in favour of the Roman way of doing things at the Synod of

Whitby. This was shortly before Theodore's arrival, and wounds had not yet healed. Remote Lindisfarne was still sympathetic to its Celtic traditions. Theodore went there and consecrated the church, dedicating it to that most Roman of patrons, St Peter himself.

Though Bede portrays Theodore as much-loved, which undoubtedly he was, he could also be very tough, and he clashed with the hot-headed St Wilfrid over the division of Wilfrid's diocese of York. Wilfrid, who wanted to keep it intact, appealed to the Pope, and went off to present his case in person. The Pope ruled in favour of Wilfrid, but by that time Theodore had already consecrated other bishops to govern the sees he meant to carve out of the York diocese. Wilfrid was, finally, restored, but with a somewhat diminished jurisdiction.

Theodore has usually been judged to have acted high-handedly, even if most agree that Wilfrid, saint though he may have been, was a difficult character with whom to deal. But behind Theodore's policy (and he set up a considerable number of new bishoprics) may have been his reading of Pope Gregory the Great's *Pastoral Care*. According to Gregory, bishops should be conscious of their dignity, but not too grand; they should, moreover, be in personal contact with the people whose spiritual welfare was their responsibility. A bishopric, therefore, should not be too small so that its incumbent was poor, nor should it be so large (as was York) that the bishop would be both rich, and incapable of close relationship with his flock.

Theodore, assisted by Abbot Adrian who had come with him from Rome and whom Theodore appointed to head the monastery of St Augustine at Canterbury, called councils and issued canons. He introduced Roman customs to the English – including music for the liturgy – and was concerned for the purity of Catholic doctrine. But when Bede recorded his long and eventful life he remembered in particular the school Theodore and Adrian had run at Canterbury, which had taught Roman law and how to work out the calendar, and had explained the Scriptures in the manner of the school at Antioch. It attracted scholars not only from England but from Ireland as well: 'Some of their students are alive today', says Bede, and 'are as proficient in Latin and Greek as in their native tongue.' In eighth-century Europe to be proficient in Greek was no small achievement.

Theodore, who had been sent to Canterbury at an age when most people today have already retired, was archbishop for over twenty years. When he died, on 19 September 690, he was at least eighty-seven years old. Not only the English Church, but Western civilization, are in his debt.

Words of St Theodore

I beseech you, dearest brethren, in the love and fear of our Saviour, to consider our faith with care, so that we may all unfailingly observe whatever our holy and venerable fathers of old laid down.

25 September

St **S**ERGIUS OF RADONEZH Few religious pictures are so likely to arouse devotion as the icons venerated by Christians of the East. But in the West we know little of the deep piety of those Churches, or of the saints who exemplified that piety by their lives. Some of them, however, are included in the general calendar of the Church, including St Sergius of Radonezh.

He was born into a noble family on 3 May 1314 and baptized Bartholomew. His parents Cyril and Mary were a devout couple, praying twice a day in their private chapel as well as attending services in the churches and monasteries of their town of Rostov. Cyril was an adviser to the Prince of Rostov, and regularly accompanied him in negotiations with the Golden Horde, the Mongol army which had recently invaded along the river Volga.

The family fortunes changed abruptly when, in 1328, the principality of Rostov was annexed to that of Moscow. They moved nearer to Moscow, to Radonezh, with their children – there were two other sons, Stephen and Peter, as well as Bartholomew. After some years in Radonezh both parents chose to enter religious life, and so did their eldest son Stephen, who had married but had been widowed. Cyril and Mary died in their respective monasteries in 1334, and at their death Bartholomew himself decided to adopt the religious life. He put himself under the direction of Stephen and together the two brothers first went to Moscow to seek the blessing of the Metropolitan and then, in the forest of Radonezh, built a wooden hermitage and a small chapel.

Stephen soon decided to rejoin a monastery so Bartholomew was alone, though visited by priests sent by the Metropolitan, or by the Abbot Mitrophanes. On 7 October 1337 Mitrophanes consecrated Bartholomew a monk, and gave him the name of Sergius: it was the feast day of Sts

Sergius and Bacchus. How long Sergius remained alone is not recorded. He passed the time cultivating his garden, reading the Scriptures, and praying. The fame of his holiness spread: others were attracted to the life in the forest, including Mitrophanes himself who, because of his years, became their superior. Sergius built them huts like his own.

After the death of Mitrophanes the monks, by now a community of twelve, elected Sergius abbot of the monastery they had named after the Most Holy Trinity. 'I would rather learn than teach', he said, 'obey than command. But I fear the judgement of God and submit to his will.' He went off with some companions to have his election confirmed by the local bishop, who at the same time ordained him priest.

Some time later the monastery was visited by representatives of the Patriarch of Constantinople. Hitherto the monks under the guidance of Sergius had lived their own lives, almost like hermits except all living in one place and meeting together for prayer. The Patriarch, on the other hand, recommended that Sergius introduce life in common. This he agreed to do, though only after consulting his own immediate superior, the Metropolitan of Moscow.

By this time the monastery had grown very much bigger, to a hundred or so monks, among them his brother Stephen who had returned with his twelve-year-old son. There was considerable discontent at the changes in religious life which Sergius was obliged to impose, and Stephen proved to be one of the more unruly members of the community. Because of the opposition, and especially it would seem that of Stephen, Sergius decided to abandon the monastery of the Most Holy Trinity and found another one. He left secretly, and established some distance away the monastery of the Annunciation, much in the way as he had his first foundation. A number of monks joined him at the Annunciation monastery: others who had stayed behind pleaded with him to return which, after four years, he agreed to do. His new foundation he left under the guidance of one of his most devoted followers, and it continued to prosper. Other foundations followed: one of them by Theodore, son of his brother Stephen, who proved to be as devout as his father was difficult, and utterly devoted to his uncle Sergius.

In all, some dozen monasteries were directly founded by Sergius or by his immediate followers, and he is looked upon as the father of Russian monasticism. It is said of him that in a vision he saw an enormous flock of birds all around the monastery and a voice told him that he would have as many disciples as the birds he had seen, and the number of those who followed him would never diminish. His monastery of the Most Holy Trinity at what is now known as Zagorsk (it eventually took the name of St Sergius himself) prospered and has continued to be a major centre both of the religious life of the people of Russia, and a national rallying-point in time of troubles.

Sergius died on 25 September 1392, aged seventy-eight. He was formally recognized as a saint in 1448.

4 October

St

RANCIS OF ASSISI Francis was born in Assisi in 1182. His father, Pietro Bernadone, was a cloth merchant. His mother was called Pica, though very little else is known about her. She may have been French, because the family had close links with France and Pietro frequently travelled there. The saint was baptized as John, but Pietro and Pica nicknamed him 'Francesco', 'the Frenchman', and the name stuck. He was not just the first St Francis, he was probably the first Francis ever.

He was romantic, passionate and poetic, roaming the streets of Assisi, singing – he was especially fond of singing, and is said to have composed music – and reciting love poetry. He wanted glory and in 1202 joined the army, but was taken prisoner and spent a year in gaol. When by 1205 he had recovered from his imprisonment he set off again, this time to join the army of the Pope. He reached Spoleto, but there he had some sort of mystical experience which sent him back to Assisi. For a time he returned to his old ways, but gradually began to discover prayer, spending hours in a deserted cave while a friend kept watch at its entrance.

One day in the church of San Damiano he heard from the crucifix before which he was praying 'Go and repair my Church'. Taking the command literally, he went about the town repairing dilapidated churches. His father was angry at Francis for squandering money in this way, and summoned him before the courts. It was the climax of the saint's conversion for, in the public square of Assisi, he handed all he had back to his father, even the clothes he was wearing. The bishop, before whom this gesture of renunciation took place, covered Francis' nakedness with his cloak.

For a while he continued repairing churches, and tending lepers in the nearby town of Gubbio but then, at mass in the little chapel called Portiuncola just outside Assisi, he heard the Gospel command in Matthew 10:7–10, to proclaim the Kingdom of heaven, to do it freely and without thought for money or clothing or even a staff. He had heard these words many times, but on 24 February 1208 they came home as never before. He threw away his staff and sandals as the Gospel directed, tying a rope about his waist in place of his leather belt. When he had gathered a small number of companions and drawn up a Rule, he put at its centre devotion to 'Lady Poverty'.

In so doing he committed himself and his followers to a radically simple style of living. But he also expected them to wander the countryside preaching the Gospel, a form of religious life which hitherto had not existed. In 1209, when Francis approached the Pope for approval of this manner of following Christ, Innocent III seems first to have hesitated, but then gave his blessing. Francis was forever grateful.

The brotherhood (and sisterhood, because St Clare joined in 1212 and other women followed her) grew rapidly. The friars went off on their preaching tours around Europe and beyond. Francis himself went to Dalmatia, France, Spain and the Holy Land. In the autumn of 1219 he talked about Christ to the Sultan at Damietta in Egypt. When he came back from this preaching tour he found an order which had grown large and complex. He resigned as its administrative head, but remained its spiritual leader and wrote for it another Rule. This was approved in 1223, and is the one Franciscans still observe.

His one desire was that he, and those who came after him, should follow Christ as closely as possible. But just how closely that could be perhaps even Francis himself had never imagined. In 1224 he was at La Verna in Tuscany – it was probably the Feast of the Exaltation of the Cross, 14 September – when he had a vision of a seraph fixed to a cross. From then onwards he bore replicas of the wounds of Christ in his hands, his feet and his side: the stigmata.

In the spring of 1225, while visiting Clare, Francis was taken seriously ill. He had been weakened by the stigmata, and was by now almost blind. It was at this time he composed the *Canticle of Brother Sun,* and had it sung by Brother Pacificus. The short poem expresses Francis' vision of creation, that all of it, from Brother Sun to Sister Moon, and from Mother Earth to Sister Death, is graced by Christ, and is united in singing the praises of God. A year later he went to Siena for treatment for his eyes, but when his health failed to improve he asked to be taken back to Assisi, to the chapel of the Portiuncola. He died, lying, at his insistence, naked upon the naked earth, in the evening of 3 October 1226. He was canonized just four years later. In 1979 he was declared by Pope John Paul to be patron saint of those with a special care for the world of nature.

A hymn based on St Francis' Canticle of the Sun

Dear mother Earth who, day by day,
Unfoldest blessings on our way,
   O praise him, Alleluia!
The flowers and fruits that in thee grow,
Let them his glory also show:
   Alleluia!

Let all things their Creator bless,
And worship him in humbleness,
   O praise him, alleluia!
Praise, praise the Father, praise the Son,
And praise the Spirit, three in One:
   Alleluia!

8 October

J OHN LEONARDI The names of several of the great reforming saints of the sixteenth century – those of Ignatius Loyola, Philip Neri, Charles Borromeo for example – are well known to Catholics. One, however, has been largely forgotten: St John Leonardi. Yet he had as much title as anyone to be included among the greatest of reformers: he did not only, like Ignatius for example, found a religious order, he was actively engaged in the work of reforming several others.

He was born at Diecimo, near Lucca in Italy, in 1541, and went to Lucca itself in 1558 to study to be a pharmacist. He was a devout young man, and chose a spiritual director from among the Dominicans in the city. He soon decided he wanted to join the Franciscans, but was rejected. He was one of a group of lay people dedicated not only to their personal spiritual advancement, but also to the care of the poor and of pilgrims. They formed a confraternity, calling themselves the 'Colombini': the first of the several religious organizations which John Leonardi had a hand in founding.

At the age of twenty-six he abandoned his profession as a pharmacist and began studies for the priesthood: he was ordained four years later. He was given charge of the church of San Giovanni della Magione, and promptly opened a school. He was particularly concerned that children should learn the Catholic faith as it had been recently formulated by the Council of Trent, and he brought his friends the Colombini in to help. Soon they were teaching catechism all round Lucca, to adults as well as to children, and a new society was founded, the Confraternity of Christian Doctrine. It quickly spread throughout Italy, and received the blessing of successive popes.

As well as instruction in doctrine, John Leonardi fostered the devotional life of those in his care. He urged upon them the practice of frequent communion, and encouraged the spread of the Forty Hours devotion. But to further this kind of work he needed the assistance of priests in addition to the laity already organized into his confraternities. In September 1574 he and a number of friends established the Confraternity of Reformed Priests of the Most Blessed Virgin: the name was changed in 1614 to the Clerks Regular of the Mother of God, by which they are still known. After its formal recognition by diocesan authorities the priests of the new congregation held their first general chapter in 1583, electing John Leonardi as their Rector.

The early years of this order, as of so many, were far from easy. They were given charge of the church of Our Lady of the Rose, but that proved too expensive to run and they moved to Our Lady Corteorlandini. Their problems arose because the wealthy families of Lucca were unwilling to support these clergy formed in the tradition of the recent Council, and successfully evangelizing the people of the city from a post-conciliar perspective. Scandalous rumours were spread about the priests, in particular about St John himself. Eventually the powerful nobles had him sent into exile: they wanted it to be a permanent exile, but the Pope of the day, Sixtus V, rejected their demands.

The exile was spent in Rome, at the service of the papacy. He became what in modern times we might call a 'troubleshooter'. First he was sent to sort out problems at a shrine in the diocese of Nola, then to Naples because there was a plague. He was asked by Pope Clement VIII to reform the congregation of Montevergine, and a few years later the order of Vallombrosa. He even had to reform his own congregation because some of its members in Lucca, during their Rector's enforced absence and because of pressure from the city magnates, had modified the rule which John Leonardi had given them.

He preached missions in dioceses at the request of local bishops and gave retreats to members of other religious congregations. One such congregation, that now known as the Piarists, even briefly amalgamated with John Leonardi's own, but it was quickly and mutually agreed that the two had quite different vocations which could not be formally linked in a single body.

In 1601 the 'Reformed Priests', as they were still called, took over a church in Rome, and John Leonardi made his home there. The young congregation was lucky in being assigned the Oratorian Cardinal Baronius as their Protector, for the famous Church historian gave them enormous support and encouragement.

The congregation was still confined to Italy, but John Leonardi very much wanted to send them to mission territories. He was dissuaded, but towards the end of his life he was involved in a starting a College in Rome whose influence has surely far outreached anything members of his own order could have done. He collaborated in founding what was later to become – under Urban VIII from whom it takes its name – the Urban College for the Propagation of the Faith which for more than 350 years has trained priests for the Church's missions.

John Leonardi died in Rome on 8 October 1609. He was beatified in 1861 and canonized in April 1938.

16 October

GERARD MAJELLA Of few saints of modern times have so many miraculous stories been told as they have of St Gerard Majella. It is said he had the gift of being in two places at once (bilocation). According to other accounts he once flew through the air a distance of half a mile. He knew what people were thinking: his reading of people's hearts brought them back to God. There seems small evidence for many of the extraordinary events related of him, but people seemed ready to believe them. He died in the night of 15–16 October 1755. Shortly afterwards, and for reasons that no one can properly explain, he was being invoked by women about to give birth, to help them during labour. More recently there have been petitions to have him declared patron saint of mothers.

He was born in April 1726. His family came from Muro near Potenza in Italy, and there he trained as a tailor. For eight years from 1736 he served in the household of the Bishop of Lacedonia. It was not a happy period. The bishop treated him severely, but he bore his anger patiently. In 1744 he returned to Muro to live with his mother, to whom he was deeply devoted, and his three sisters. Possibly it was his generosity to his mother – he gave a third of his earnings to her, and another third he distributed in alms – that won him his reputation as a patron of mothers.

Gerard had an uncle who was a Franciscan, and a man of some importance. He determined, therefore, to follow his uncle's example and join the order. They would not have him. Then the Redemptorists, newly founded by St Alphonsus Liguori, came to Muro to preach a parish mission. Gerard was deeply moved. He determined to join them, but the Redemptorists, too, were not eager to have him, and his family was loath to lose him. When the Redemptorists grudgingly gave in, he had to flee secretly from his family.

The initial reluctance to accept the poor tailor of Muro was rapidly replaced by a recognition of the sanctity which he had already achieved. St Alphonsus himself reduced the length of time Gerard was required to spend in the novitiate. He was professed as a lay brother on 16 July 1752. To the traditional vows of poverty, chastity and obedience he added one more: always to do that which was more pleasing to God.

As a lay brother he took on many tasks. He was, of course, a tailor to the community, but he was also in turn cook and sacristan, doorkeeper and infirmarian. There was nothing he was not prepared to do in the service of his Master. He took charge for a time of the finances, and there was no one better at begging for money from the rich families of the neighbourhood. Indeed, they seem to have encouraged him, for as he went from house to house he resolved squabbles and reconciled sinners. Strangest of all, perhaps because he had so great a reputation for holiness himself, he was put in charge of the spiritual direction of nuns, something then unheard of for lay brothers.

On one occasion a woman accused him of making advances. He refused to defend himself from the groundless accusation and was therefore sent away to Naples, serving in several Redemptorist houses. It was there in particular that his fame as a healer began to spread, and crowds came to him to beg his help in their illnesses.

He retired from Naples to Caposele to be away from the crowds. He was made doorkeeper, and the crowds kept coming. He was then put in charge of the new building operations at Caposele: his reputation as a fundraiser had gone before him. This time, however, his work in raising money cost him his life. During the summer of 1755 he wandered through southern Italy seeking money. The southern heat proved too much and he had to spend a week in bed. He dragged himself back to Caposele, and died there some six weeks later. Ever the miracle-worker, it is said he foretold both the day and the time of his death. He was canonized in 1904.

A prayer of St Gerard Majella

O Lord, thou seest that I have not forgotten thee. It is now for thee to think of me.

30 October

St

A LPHONSUS RODRIGUEZ Alphonsus was born in Segovia, Spain, about the year 1533. His father Diego was a prosperous wool merchant, his mother was Maria Gomez. They had four daughters and seven sons, of whom Alphonsus was the second. It was a devout household, and when Pierre Favre, one of Ignatius Loyola's first companions, came to Segovia to preach he stayed with Diego, and afterwards spent a few days at the family's country house, accompanied by Alphonsus.

At the age of ten or eleven he went to study at Alcalá where the Jesuits had recently founded a college. His education was cut short. In 1545 his father died, and his mother called him (and not his elder brother who was also in the college) home to help run the business. Ten years or so later his mother retired: at the age of twenty-three he was left in sole charge.

Some time about 1560 he married Maria Suarez, possibly so that her dowry might help prop up his ailing business. They had two children, a girl and a boy. But first his daughter died, and then, after a long illness, so did Maria. Alphonsus gave up the struggle to keep his firm going and with his young son moved back to his mother's house. But then his son died.

Alphonsus was a pious man – indeed, biographers have sometimes attributed the decline in his fortunes to his scrupulous honesty – and it was not surprising that he should think of joining a religious order. He went to see the Jesuits in Segovia but they would not have him. Their decision was understandable. Though they might have been impressed by his practice of morning and evening meditation, by the austerity of his life and by his weekly confession and communion, as a widower and a failed business man he was not a typical candidate. More to the point, he was nearly forty and his formal education was sadly deficient.

He determined to remedy his lack of Latin and in Valencia sat down to learn among schoolboys. He had no money and lived partly on alms and later worked as a servant. He was tempted briefly by the life of a hermit but then again applied to join the Jesuits. Once more the Provincial's advisers turned him down but the Provincial himself, Fr Cordeses, decided otherwise. He was admitted to the noviceship as a candidate lay brother on 31 January 1571, and took his vows as a Jesuit on 5 April 1573. During the noviceship and for long afterwards he felt insecure in his vocation, believing himself to be on the verge of dismissal from the Society. In 1585, however, he made his final vows. He was fifty-four years old.

Six months later he was sent to Majorca. He arrived in Palma on 10 August 1573 and remained there until his death on 30 October 1617. And for those forty-four years he had but one task: 'In Majorca Alfonso watched the door' of the Jesuit College of Montesión, as Gerard Manley Hopkins wrote of him.

He had a great devotion to Our Lady's Immaculate Conception, saw visions and had other mystical experiences, but it was the day-by-day commitment to his job as porter for which he has been remembered. He wrote his own rules, telling himself that he must welcome each caller as if God himself. He talked to those who passed in and out, and many took him for their spiritual guide. One who did so was Peter Claver, who came to the College in 1605 and to whom he gave the advice to go to work in the Americas.

Alphonsus was no plaster-cast saint. He had constantly to fight temptation, particularly temptations against chastity. He was obedient, sometimes almost foolishly so, if the stories are to be believed. But he was deeply loved both by his community and by the people of Majorca. They came in crowds to the funeral, from the Viceroy to the poorest, and made him patron of the island in 1633, long before his canonization. That came on 15 January 1888, with his former disciple in the spirit, St Peter Claver.

A thought of St Alphonsus Rodriguez

To try to know oneself is the foundation of everything. He who knows himself despises himself, while he who does not know himself is puffed up.

St

ARTIN DE PORRES It is, unhappily, to their shame that there used to exist in religious orders a ban on admitting to membership people born outside of marriage, or who were not of European origin. These were rules which could be, and often were, waived by ecclesiastical superiors. St Martin was not refused entry to the Dominicans when he requested it, but was given the lowest of positions: he was admitted not as a priest or lay brother, but as a 'lay helper'. His father was furious, and urged him to change his mind about joining the friars, but he remained firm. It was when he was fifteen years old that he joined the Order of Preachers, in the Convent of the Most Holy Rosary in Lima, Peru.

His father was a Spanish nobleman, Juan de Porres, Knight of the Order of Alcantara, living, at the time of Martin's birth on 9 December 1579, in Lima. Martin's mother, Anna Vasquez, was from Panama, but of a family which had originally come from Africa. It is said that Juan de Porres disowned his son when he saw the dark colour of his skin. Certainly he was entered into the baptismal register as 'father unknown' and for a number of years he and his sister, who was two years younger, lived with Anna in Lima and apart from their father. When Martin was eight, however, Juan sent for the two children to come to him in Ecuador. They stayed for five years while Martin went to school, but when his father was appointed governor of Panama the children were separated. Martin went back to Lima, supported financially by his father so that he might continue his education, and learn a trade. The trade he chose was that of 'barber-surgeon', a curious mixture of barber, pharmacist and doctor, at which he became well skilled, and, while still very young, gained a considerable reputation throughout Lima, especially among the poor.

As a Dominican he put his medical skills at the service of his brethren, serving them with great patience and gentleness. He was renowned for his humility. At one point, when the finances of the convent were at a particularly low ebb, he suggested that the convent might sell him into slavery to raise much-needed funds. His proposal was rejected. As time went by, the community became increasingly impressed by Martin's holiness of life. Nine years after he had entered, they asked him to take the vows they had refused him when he entered. Martin at first said no, but the friars insisted, and he made his profession as a Dominican lay brother on 2 June 1603.

Martin's life went on much as before. Because of his mixed race he felt himself to have a special apostolate to those like himself, and to those, slave or free, who were of the same background as his mother. He was also a man whose reputation for wisdom far outstripped his formal education, and he was consulted by the rich as well as by the poor. It was to the poor, however, and especially the poor children of Lima, that he showed greatest sympathy. He had built for them the College of the Holy Cross, the first hospital of its kind in the New World.

His life was full of quite extraordinary events. He would spend long hours in front of the Blessed Sacrament, rapt in ecstasy. One of his fellow Dominicans testified after his death that he had often seen him in prayer in the chapel, lifted off his feet and brought close up to the crucifix on the altar. It was said that he could be in two places at once, that he could cure people miraculously, that he had visions, and that his theological knowledge (it was claimed that he knew not only the whole of Scripture but even the *Summa Theologiae* of St Thomas Aquinas) came directly from God.

And then there was his friendship with animals, in which

he rivalled St Francis. All animals approached him without fear, and he talked to them as he would to men and women. But he had a particular care of animals which others despised or ignored: he was especially attracted to rats. He is sometimes invoked against plagues of rats because, on one occasion, he is said to have gathered all the rats in a sacristy up in a basket, and carried them far away from the church.

When he was in his sixtieth year, the new Archbishop of Mexico, who had been cured by Martin, asked if the saint could join him in Mexico City. It would take him away, he argued, from the danger of pride in the reputation he had built up. Martin's Dominican superiors agreed, but he died, on 3 November 1639, before he was forced to leave the city.

4 November

HARLES BORROMEO The Council of Trent took place over a long drawn-out period in the middle of the sixteenth century. It reformed Church structures and formulated doctrines about the essentials of the Catholic faith. One of its greatest achievements was to order the establishment of colleges for the training of clergy so that the priests of the seventeenth and subsequent centuries were much better educated in theology than most of their predecessors. It was one thing to decree reforms, quite another to put them into practice. They might have remained a dead letter had it not been for the zeal of some remarkable men and women who reformed their religious orders, started new ones, or brought back their dioceses to a renewed zeal for the Christian life. Chief among these is Charles Borromeo, called by one biographer 'the Prince of Pastors'.

Charles was not literally a prince, but very nearly so. His father was a Count, his mother a member of the Medici family, and he was born in a castle on Lake Maggiore on 2 October 1538. He was a devout boy in a devout household, though the fact that, at the age of twelve, he set out on a clerical career probably had more to do with safeguarding the family fortunes than with any piety he may have displayed. He went to the University at Pavia and gained a doctorate but was not especially outstanding as a scholar, and his natural hesitancy suggested that he was not cut out for high office.

Then one of his Medici uncles was elected Pope Pius IV. That was in 1559. Early the following year Pius created his nephew a cardinal deacon, and heaped upon him all manner of honours and responsibilities, including the administration of the diocese of Milan. Charles wanted to take this last task seriously, but Pius detained him in Rome, relying upon him for help in summoning a final session of the Council of Trent. Charles played a central role, holding the Council together, and ensuring that the important disciplinary and dogmatic decrees of the final session were eventually approved by the bishops. As the Council began he was still only in deacon's orders. When Count Borromeo died Charles became head of the family but resigned that position to an uncle. He was ordained priest in 1564, and made a bishop only two months later, but was still not allowed to take charge of his diocese. He was obliged to stay on in Rome to assist in the reform of the liturgy, and to help to produce the 'Roman Catechism' which summed up the teachings of Trent. In 1565, however, his uncle Pius IV died, and the new pontiff, Pope Pius V, permitted him to move to Milan, a city which had not seen a resident bishop (such as the decrees of Trent required) for eighty years. He arrived there in April 1566.

It was precisely the reforms instituted by Trent that he attempted to introduce to Milan. They were not always welcome: one priest tried to shoot the archbishop as he knelt in prayer in his private chapel. One of the ways in which the saint commended his reforms to others was by the personal holiness, and austerity, of his life. He was immensely rich, but he gave away vast sums of money and lived a very simple life. His generosity was especially welcome during the famine of 1570. During the epidemic of the plague from 1576 to 1578 he nursed the sick and visited the dying with no concern for his own safety.

Education was his first priority. He opened three seminaries to serve the needs of his clergy. He also began a Confraternity of Christian Doctrine in the city, and instituted the practice of Sunday schools. He recognized that a better educated clergy would be restless unless they were involved in running the diocese, and he began, again in line with Trent, a series of diocesan synods where their views were sought. One of the seminaries he helped to assist financially was that of the English College at Douay. He seemed indeed to have an particular affinity to the British: he chose a Welshman as his confessor and, among many other visitors, welcomed the future martyrs Ralph Sherwin and Edmund Campion as they made their way to England and to death.

Charles' own death came on the night of 3–4 November 1584 after a short illness. He was buried in the cathedral of Milan and the people of his city promptly hailed him as a saint. Official recognition soon followed: he was canonized in 1610.

Words of St Charles Borromeo

> Whoever would go forward in God's service must begin life anew each day, must keep as much as possible in the presence of God, and in all must have but one object, God's glory.

15 November

St A

LBERT THE GREAT It was the practice of writers in the later Middle Ages to give nicknames to their more illustrious predecessors. One was known as 'the angelical Doctor', for example, another 'the subtle Doctor'. Albert of Lauingen was simply known, and even to his contemporaries, as 'the great'.

Lauingen is a small town between Ulm and Regensburg in what is now Germany. About Albert's childhood little or nothing is known, not even the date of his birth though it was probably about the year 1193. His father was possibly a high-ranking soldier with responsibility for the region of Lauingen: certainly the family must have been fairly wealthy, for Albert travelled (the earliest certain date in his life is 1222 when he says he witnessed earthquakes in northern Italy) and became a student at the newly-opened University of Padua.

It is not even certain when he first joined the Order of Preachers, the Dominicans. Blessed Jordan of Saxony formally received him into the order, however, in 1229 and sent him to Cologne, the most important house of studies for the Dominicans in the whole of Germany. That same year the Dominicans were granted for the first time a chair of theology at the University of Paris, so it was to Paris that Albert went in 1242 to prepare for his doctorate. He already had a reputation for great learning and one of his students, Thomas Aquinas, followed him to Paris.

After Albert gained his doctorate and Thomas his bachelor's degree both were sent back to Cologne to take charge of the Dominican house of studies. Albert was in overall charge, Thomas, under him, looked after the students. It is likely that as early as 1238 Albert had almost been elected to take charge of the whole order, for he had a reputation which went far beyond that simply of a learned man. While at

Cologne he mediated for the first time in a quarrel in the city
– on this occasion between the citizens and the archbishop.
His skills as an administrator were recognized when, in 1254,
he was elected as Provincial for an area which embraced all
the German-speaking lands and even included what are now
Holland and Belgium, parts of Poland and districts as far
north as Latvia.

These were crowded years for the new Provincial. His
order was expanding rapidly, especially his own province.
The post entailed incessant journeyings and his visitations
may have taken him right up to Riga. But as well as success
there were setbacks. The Dominicans, along with the
Franciscans, were under attack. A teacher at the University of
Paris wrote a book on *The Dangers of the Present Age* in which
he singled out for criticism the role of the friars in the universities. Albert went to the papal court, then at Anagni, to
defend his brethren's rights. He was accompanied again by
Thomas Aquinas, and also by the Franciscan Bonaventure.
Against the arguments of three men, all eventually to be
acknowledged as saints, the campaign against the friars stood
no chance: their right to hold university posts was upheld.

While in Anagni Albert's abilities as a theologian were
recognized by Pope Alexander IV, who appointed him
'Master of the Sacred Palace'. This made him an adviser to
the Pope on theological matters, and a papal preacher both in
Anagni and in Rome. His period as Provincial came to an
end in 1258, and he returned for a while to his post in charge
of the Dominican house in Cologne. Two years later, however,
the Pope chose him as Bishop of Regensburg where Albert
swiftly put his administrative skills to good use in improving
the finances of the diocese, and then in reorganizing the religious houses and parishes. That done, in less than two years he
resigned, and went back to writing, teaching and preaching.

His skills as a preacher were called upon when Pope Urban

IV asked him to raise money for a possible crusade, and to aid the Holy Land. His abilities as a mediator were frequently sought after – at least twice more by the citizens of Cologne as well as by others. He continued his teaching until 1278, by which time he was almost certainly more than eighty years old: the year before he had travelled to Paris to defend his former pupil Thomas, who had died in 1274, against charges of teaching heresy. And all the time he kept up an extraordinary flow of writings on a range of subjects which included geography and astronomy as well as philosophy and theology.

He died quietly in his cell at Cologne on 15 November 1280. His reputation for sanctity was widespread in Germany. Although he was eventually beatified in 1622, he has never formally been canonized. Except indirectly, that is, for in December 1931 Pope Pius XI declared him to be a Doctor of the Church.

A prayer of St Albert the Great

> Lord Jesus Christ, listen to my voice rising to you from the bleak valley of repentance. I beseech you that I may not be led astray by the temptations of empty words that speak of family pride, of the prestige of my order, of the pleasures of knowledge.

28 November

ATHERINE LABOURÉ The feasts are kept, almost exactly a month apart, of two saints in whose public lives little remarkable happened, and who within their religious communities performed the same humdrum task of door-keeper. St Alphonsus Rodriguez is celebrated on 30 October, St Catherine Labouré on 28 November.

Catherine was her name as a Sister of Charity of St Vincent de Paul: she was born in Fain-les-Moutiers, a village in Burgundy, on 2 May 1806 and baptized Zoé. When she was nine her mother died and three years later her sister, Marie Louise, left home to join the Sisters of Charity. Many of the family responsibilities, and those of her father's farm, now fell to Zoé. She performed them well, but her deepest desire was to imitate Marie Louise. This her father at first refused to let her do. To distract her he sent her to Paris, in the care of her brother Charles, and then to a boarding school at Châtillon-sur-Seine where her sister-in-law was headmistress. When she remained adamant he relented a little, but refused to provide the dowry required by the convent. Her sister-in-law paid it instead.

So it was at Châtillon early in 1830 that she joined the Sisters of Charity as a postulant, and as a novice went to the Paris convent at rue de Bac on 21 April that year. The apparitions which made her famous began almost at once. She had arrived just as the relics of St Vincent de Paul were about to be solemnly moved to the church of St Lazare. When she returned from a visit to her community's chapel she saw the heart of St Vincent hovering above some relics which were on the altar. Afterwards, she told her confessor, Fr Aladel, she saw visions of Christ in the Blessed Sacrament. On the night of 18 July Catherine was roused from her sleep by a small

child who took her down to the chapel. There she received
her first vision of the Virgin Mary. It lasted two hours, and
Mary's warnings of disasters to come for France were amply
fulfilled by the revolution which shortly afterwards overthrew
King Charles X.

The most famous vision occurred in the same small chapel
on 27 November. Mary appeared as if in a picture, standing
upon a globe with a serpent under her foot. Light streamed
from her hands and around her was the prayer 'O Mary, con-
ceived without sin, pray for us who have recourse to thee'.
The image was reversed. It now showed a letter M, through
which ran a bar, and upon the bar a cross. Twelve stars sur-
rounded the M, and beneath it were two hearts, one pierced
with a sword, the other crowned with thorns. A voice
instructed her to have a medal struck bearing these symbols,
promising great graces to anyone who would wear it about
their neck.

Catherine Labouré told Fr Aladel and he told the
Archbishop of Paris: in June 1832 the first 1,500 'miraculous
medals' were issued. A tribunal, before which Sister Catherine
refused to appear, declared the visions authentic. Belief in the
power of the medal was enormously increased through the
sudden conversion to Catholicism of Alphonse Ratisbonne
in the Roman church of Sant' Andrea delle Fratte: he had
been persuaded to wear it during his visit. Ratisbonne, a Jew,
went on to found the Sisters of Sion who work for understanding between Jews and Christians.

There were other visions of Mary. They lasted until
September 1831. But then Catherine, her noviceship being
over, was sent to work in the Hospice of Enghien, also in
Paris, and the apparitions came to an end. All this time,
though the visions were talked about, the identity of the seer
was never revealed. Catherine lived quietly at the hospice,
looking after the old, feeding the poultry, and taking charge

of the door. Among those who knew her, nuns and clergy, she had a reputation for holiness. There were rumours that she was the visionary of the rue de Bac, but she spoke of what she had seen only to her superior and then not until the very end of her life.

Her years as a Sister of Charity were quiet ones, disturbed only briefly by the Franco-Prussian War and the Paris Commune. She died at Enghien on 31 December 1876 and was buried there on 3 January. She was canonized on 12 July 1947, and her remains now rest in the chapel where she received her visions. Her feast was set not for the day of her death, but on 28 November, to mark the revelation of the Miraculous Medal.

St

LOI (OR ELIGIUS) The exact date of Eloi's birth is uncertain, but it was about the year 590. He was born in Chaptelat, a small town just north of Limoges, to parents of modest means who, when he was old enough, sent him to Lyons as an apprentice to the smith who had charge of the royal mint. He then transferred to Paris in the service of the royal treasurer who introduced him to the King. Clotar II commissioned him to make a golden throne and Eloi did so, but found he had material to spare and so made two thrones instead of one. Clotar was impressed, perhaps as much by Eloi's honesty as his skill, and took him into the royal service. A number of Eloi's commissions are known, though none that are certainly his have survived to the present day – one, a chalice, disappeared only during the French Revolution. He became director of the mint at Marseilles, and coins have been preserved from that period of his life.

Under Clotar's son and successor Dagobert I Eloi continued to flourish. He was asked to coin medals and make other objects, but in addition, such was his reputation for honesty, he was given special tasks by the King. He had a particular concern for prisoners of war who were held as slaves, and worked for their release from bondage.

By this time he had become wealthy, and about the year 632 he used some of his riches to found an abbey at Solignac, just south of Limoges, on land given him by the King. It was a monastery for men, and it followed a rule of life which drew upon the rules of both St Benedict and St Columbanus. The year after he founded another monastery at Paris, this time for women, again on an estate which had been a royal gift. His generosity was legendary. When some stranger asked the way to Eloi's house he was told 'Where you see a crowd of poor people, that is where Eloi lives'.

After Dagobert's death in 639 he decided to leave the court and become a priest. In 641 he was chosen as Bishop of Noyon in Northern France. He founded several monasteries in his diocese, which extended into what is now Belgium, and travelled continuously around his diocese, preaching the gospel to his people and winning converts to Christianity. St Ouen, the former chancellor of King Dagobert, became Bishop of Rouen the same year that Eloi went to Noyon and the two worked together evangelizing the countryside. One who helped them was Tillo, a Saxon redeemed from slavery by Eloi, who had become a monk at Solignac.

Even after Eloi had become a bishop he remained a royal counsellor. He was particularly close to Bathildis, the Queen Regent, an Anglo-Saxon who had been sold as a slave in her childhood. Eloi and Bathildis are credited with a decree of the Council of Chalon, held about the year 647, which forbade the sale of slaves out of the kingdom, and ordered that they be allowed a day of rest on Sundays.

Eloi died in 660, probably on 1 December, the day which has been celebrated as his feast since the Middle Ages. Though he was particularly popular in France, he also was venerated across Europe as patron of all those trades, from goldsmiths to blacksmiths, concerned in metalwork. He is also patron saint of horses because of something supposed to have happened after his death. Eloi bequeathed his horse to a priest of Noyon, but the animal was taken over, quite wrongly, by his successor as bishop. The horse fell ill, and the bishop, having no use for a sick horse, returned it to the priest – whereupon it promptly recovered its health.

St

RANCIS XAVIER In 1927 Pope Pius XI proclaimed two saints as patrons of the Church's missionary activity. One of them, Thérèse of the Child Jesus, a Carmelite nun, had prayed for those who worked in the mission fields. The other was St Francis Xavier.

The simple facts of Francis' birth and death bear witness to his extraordinary achievements in proclaiming the message of Christ. He was born into a noble family, in the castle of Javier (or Xavier) in Navarre on 7 April 1506. His father, Juan de Yasu, held a doctorate from the University of Bologna, and was a member of the royal council. His mother Maria was of the ancient nobility of the region. When he died, on 3 December 1552, he was practically alone, poverty-stricken, and on the island of Sancian, just off the coast of China. In between the castle of Javier and the island close to China he had lived out one of the most remarkable lives of any sixteenth-century Christian.

His adventures began as if by chance. After studying in Spain he went in 1525 to the College of Sainte-Barbe in Paris. In 1526 he began sharing lodgings with Pierre Favre and, from 1529, with Ignatius Loyola. Pierre soon fell under the influence of Ignatius, but the sporty Francis was more resistant to Ignatius' appeal that he should give up everything to follow Christ. By 1533, however, Francis had been won over, and on 15 August 1534 Ignatius, Pierre Favre, Francis Xavier and four others took a vow in a chapel on Montmartre to commit themselves to the service of God in a life of poverty and chastity, and – as Ignatius had already done – to go on pilgrimage to the Holy Land.

This last part of their vow these first Jesuits (their order received verbal approval from the Pope in September 1539) found impossible to fulfil. They went instead by stages to Rome, and put themselves at the service of the Pope. Even before the Society of Jesus was formally approved, Francis had set off on his missionary journeys. He was not Ignatius' first choice when King John III of Portugal asked for someone to minister to the Christians of the Portuguese territories in India. But the man originally chosen was ill, so Francis went in his place – and never returned to Europe.

Before he could take ship for India he had to spend nine months in Lisbon, time spent in teaching catechism and hearing confessions. When he eventually set sail, in April 1541, the journey to Goa took thirteen months. In Goa he struggled to learn the language so as to preach and hear confessions. He also translated a catechism. His mission was both to the Portuguese colonists – Goa was the capital of the Portuguese empire in the East – and to the local peoples who had been converted to Catholicism before Francis' arrival, but whose faith had lapsed through lack of priests to minister to them. Francis believed, as did everyone else at the time, that those who were not baptized could not be saved, a belief which lent great urgency to his efforts. So worn out was he by administering so many baptisms, he wrote back to Europe in January 1544, that he could scarcely raise his right arm.

He worked for two years on the Pearl Fishery Coast, opposite what is now Sri Lanka. He had, he noted, considerable success with the people of a lower caste but almost none at all with high-caste Brahmins. He had problems from non-Christians, who on one occasion slaughtered six hundred of his converts, and took others off into slavery. He had even worse problems from the appalling example of brutality and drunkenness given by the Portuguese merchants and government officials.

It is impossible in a short space to recount all the saint's travels. They took him to the Malay peninsula and to the Moluccas. In Malacca in 1547 he met a Japanese who was fleeing his own country because of a charge of murder against him. Francis was fired with a desire to go there, but it was not until August 1549 that he finally landed in southern Japan, accompanied by a small group of Jesuits. Again there was the problem of learning a new language and translating a catechism. Progress was at first extremely slow, and Francis came to the conclusion that the apostolic poverty was not suitable for impressing Japanese society: to win acceptance he put on better clothes and gave expensive presents. He went in their door, he said of the Japanese, so that they might come out of his. It was a policy adopted with extraordinary success by those who followed him in the mission fields of the Far East.

In Japan he heard a great deal about the great civilization of China. He was determined to make his way there. After just over two years in Japan he returned to Goa to prepare to go to China. He was trying to arrange entry into that country when he was taken ill with a fever. After his death his body was brought back to Goa, where it is still venerated. He was canonized in 1622.

Many people have believed that this beautiful hymn is by St Francis Xavier, though it is not certain.

My God, I love thee, not because
   I hope for heaven thereby,
Nor yet because who love thee not
   Are lost eternally.

Not with the hope of gaining aught,
   Or seeking a reward;
But as thy self hast loved me,
   O ever-loving Lord.

14 December

St J OHN OF THE CROSS There have been poets who were priests; there have been poets who were mystics. John of the Cross is unique in being priest, saint, mystic, Doctor of the Church, and not simply a poet but one of the greatest in the Spanish language. His poems express the difficult, terrifying experience of approaching union with God through what he called the 'dark night of the soul'. The prose works for which he is remembered are in effect commentaries on his poetry.

John was born in the village of Fontiveros, not far from Avila, in 1542: his father Gonzalo de Yepes was of a noble family of Toledo which had fallen on hard times. Gonzalo died when John was about two-and-a-half, and the family moved house – eventually to Medina del Campo. There John was supported by a rich patron, also originally from Toledo, and was able to attend the Jesuit school in that city. In 1563 he left school and became a Carmelite friar. The following year he was sent to the University in Salamanca, and he was ordained priest in the summer of 1567.

It was about the time of his ordination that John met St Teresa of Avila. Teresa had already begun the reform of the Carmelite order. She had established 'discalced' (the word means 'barefoot') Carmelite convents where the nuns followed the order's original rule. She had also obtained permission to open two houses of Discalced Carmelites for men. John was not quite her first recruit to this new enterprise, but he was by far the most significant, and the one to whom Teresa felt most drawn. 'He may be short in stature', she wrote of him, 'but I believe him to be very great in the eyes of God.'

A house was provided for the friars of the reform in the village of Duruelo. The place was so poor and dirty that Teresa had doubts about its suitability. John, by this time known by his religious title as John of the Cross, arrived there in September 1568 and started putting the house in order. More recruits came: John was their master of novices. His regime was so strict and penitential that Teresa tried to mitigate the friars' asceticism. In 1572 he was appointed confessor to the Convent of the Incarnation in Avila, the house Teresa had first joined and to which, for some of the time when John was confessor, she came back as prioress. It was John, at least as much as Teresa, who transformed the hitherto rather lax regime of the nuns into one of deep religious fervour.

Tension between Carmelites of the old rule and of the new grew in intensity over these years. John was acknowledged as a leader of the reform, and members of the old observance tried to persuade him to give up his commitment to the discalced branch of the Order. He steadfastly refused, but when a General Chapter of the Carmelites rejected the reform, and denied the discalced their independence, a group of friars of the old observance broke into John's house in Avila and kidnapped him.

That was in December 1577. For more than eight months he was kept in a tiny cell with little food, no change of clothing, and no window on to the world outside. It was during this period that he wrote his greatest poetry, when he had nothing to distract him from his meditation upon God, and the approach of the soul to God. Shortly after the Feast of the Assumption, 1578, John escaped from prison, taking with him the notebooks containing his poetry. The escape has sometimes been presented as miraculous, but it probably happened with the connivance of his gaoler.

It was in the year immediately following his escape that he wrote his most important works of mystical theology, *The Ascent of Mount Carmel* and *The Dark Night of the Soul*. The person seeking union with God has to be detached, said St John, from everything in this world. That is the first 'night'.

The second night is the coming of God into the soul which, having not yet reached perfection, becomes dark because human reason cannot understand. These may have been deep matters of theology, which earned him in 1926 the title of 'Doctor of the Church', but he was admired by those who knew him for the warmth of his character and for the simplicity of his spiritual direction, especially of the nuns under his charge.

After his escape he held important posts in different houses of the Reform he had initiated, but his final years – he died when he was only 49 – were saddened by dissension among the Discalced Carmelites themselves. John of the Cross was stripped of all authority and banished to the house at Ubeda where he died, on the night of 13–14 December 1591. He was canonized in 1726.

A prayer of St John of the Cross

Mine are the heavens and mine is the earth. Mine are the nations; the just are mine and the sinners are mine. The angels are mine and the Mother of God and all things are mine. And God himself is mine and all for me, because Christ is mine and all for me.

21 December

St

THOMAS THE APOSTLE The Apostles were the foundation upon which, after Christ himself, the Church was built. The Church was the 'new Israel', which is why Jesus chose precisely twelve people out of all his many disciples, and why, after Judas' defection and death, the remaining Apostles quickly selected someone else to make up their number. Yet it is extraordinary, given their central role, how very little we know about them. Even Peter, their undisputed leader, suddenly disappears from the Acts of the Apostles and nothing more is heard of him – apart, of course, from legends which grew up later. Of all the Apostles except for Peter himself, perhaps the one whose personality emerges most clearly in the Gospels is St Thomas, whose feast is celebrated on 21 December. Again, nothing but legends survive about what happened to him after the Ascension, yet his character is well defined.

The fourth Gospel mentions him four times. In the first instance, Jesus is urged to go back to Bethany where Lazarus has just died. It is a dangerous thing to do, because Bethany is not far from Jerusalem from which he has just been driven out. When Jesus decides he will go, Thomas seems to be reconciled to the risk. 'Let us go and die with him', he tells the others.

The second occasion is in the Upper Room, during the Last Supper. Jesus tells his Apostles that he is going away, and that they know where. Perhaps they were all as puzzled as Thomas, but it is Thomas who bluntly voices their ignorance, and elicits Jesus' response 'I am the way ...'.

The third and fourth occasions are really part of the same story, the one for which Thomas is best known, and which has given rise to the expression 'doubting Thomas'. When Jesus first appears to the Apostles in the Upper Room after the Resurrection, Thomas is not present. When the other Apostles excitedly tell him what he happened, he quite properly refuses to be convinced. Unless he sees the wounds of the nails in the hands of Christ, unless he sees the wound in Christ's side, he will not believe.

In that agnostic state he remained for a week. One can imagine that it made his companions feel uncomfortable and perhaps even dampened their own enthusiasm when they could not persuade him of what they had experienced. Then Jesus again came to visit the Upper Room, this time when Thomas was present. Jesus passed no judgement on Thomas' doubts. He accepted them for what they were, and let Thomas carry out the tests which, he had said, would convince him of the truth of the Resurrection. Jesus called to him to put his fingers in the wounds in his hands and side. Thomas did so, and believed. For that, Jesus said he was blessed but, he added, even more blessed are those who have not seen but yet have believed.

Thomas was present at the miraculous catch of fish on Lake Galilee, he was present in the Upper Room when Matthias was chosen to replace Judas. He is always mentioned in the lists of Apostles as they occur in the Gospels. But that is all. What he, or any of the Apostles, did with the rest of their lives is recorded only in legend.

The legend of St Thomas, however, is particularly colourful, though there are some who believe it may contain the tiniest grain of truth. According to the Acts of Thomas, the Apostles decided that each should take some particular part of the world in which to spread the gospel. They drew lots, and to Thomas fell the task of converting India. For this role the saint felt entirely inadequate, but then Jesus himself took a hand. The 'King of the Indians', Gundaphorus, needed a carpenter to assist in building a house, and sent one of his officials to find one in Jerusalem. Jesus encountered this official, and pretending that Thomas was his slave and a carpenter, sold him to the official (his name was Abban). So Thomas went to India and set about preaching the Gospel. He had many adventures, and finally died a martyr's death there, though his bones were removed from his Indian grave and taken back to the West: Edessa has claimed them from very early times. Whatever the truth of this story – and Gundaphorus is an historical character from the first Christian century – the St Thomas Christians of India's Malabar coast claim him as their apostle and founder.

In the Middle Ages Thomas was frequently portrayed as a carpenter, and he came to be regarded as the patron of carpenters and architects. But today, with his desire to see firm evidence, this blunt, loyal follower of Jesus would perhaps more suitably be the patron saint of journalism or of the police.

Words of St John Chrysostom about Thomas

He who once saw danger in the short journey to Bethany, now, full of courage, carries the faith further than any of the other apostles.

22 December

St F RANCES XAVIER CABRINI It was once said of Frances Xavier Cabrini that if Christopher Columbus had discovered America, Mother Frances had discovered all the Italians in America. In 1950 Pius XII made her patron saint of all immigrants; two years later the American Committee for Italian Immigration declared her the 'Immigrant of the Century', and awarded a diploma to prove it. Canonized in 1946, she was the first citizen of the United States (she became one in 1909) to be made a saint.

She was born on 15 July 1850, the last of thirteen children of Agostino Cabrini and Stella Oldini, and baptized with the names Maria Francesca. Her family was relatively prosperous – Agostino owned and farmed land in Lombardy. It was also pious: Francesca had a priest uncle who was renowned for his holiness of life.

From her early years Francesca wanted to be a missionary, in particular a missionary to China. She even gave up sweets to prepare herself for life in China without them. Her parents, however, decided otherwise and sent her to a convent boarding school so that she might become a teacher. In 1870 her parents died within ten months of each other, and for two years she lived quietly with her sister Rosa. Then for a further two years she taught at Vidardo.

Her work impressed the parish priest of that town and, when he was moved to Codogno and found himself with responsibility for an orphanage which was being particularly badly managed, he pressed Francesca to take it in hand. This she did in 1874, becoming a nun three years later and taking charge of the 'House of Providence' as the first superior of a new religious congregation. The struggle to save the orphanage was unsuccessful. The Bishop of Lodi closed it. But he knew of Francesca's desire to go to China: 'I do not know of any institute of missionary nuns', he told her, 'Found one yourself.' With the seven women who had taken vows with her in 1877 she set up a new house, and a new name for her institute. She called them the Missionary Sisters of the Sacred Heart, with the Christian education of girls as its principal purpose. With that purpose no one could have any quarrel. It was much more difficult for her to retain the word 'missionary' in the title of her congregation, for such a role for women was practically unknown in the Church.

She was determined to hold to her original intention. The name of her congregation survived, and on 25 September 1887, before the altar of St Francis Xavier in the Jesuit church of the Gesù in Rome, she and six of her nuns took a vow to go to China. To reserve her recruits for that purpose she had restricted her foundations, despite the growing number who wished to join her. In 1888, when opening a house in Piacenza, she met Bishop Giovanni Scalabrini who was already sending priests to work among Italian immigrants in New York. He urged her to go there. She wavered, and consulted Leo XIII: 'Your China will be the United States', he said, and freed her from her vow to travel east. She and six of her sisters arrived in New York on 31 March 1889, only three weeks after her interview with Pope Leo. Four months later she was able to make her first return visit to Italy with two American recruits to her congregation.

At first she was hampered by her English, which she spoke to the end of her life with a strong Italian accent, and by an initial distaste for non-Catholics, with whom, in the United States, she came into contact for the first time. But these hindrances did not stand in the way of an extraordinary life of constant voyaging by land and sea and – over the Andes at some considerable risk – by mule. Her style was quick and business-like, especially where money was concerned. Her first foundation across the Atlantic was an orphanage. Others followed: schools, hospitals, clinics in North, Central and South America. She made time to visit France and, in 1898, England. In the Americas her fame was widespread: the prisoners of Sing Sing sent an illuminated address.

Her death came suddenly, when she was alone. She died on 22 December 1917 and was beatified less than a dozen years after her death.

St Frances Cabrini's advice to her nuns

> Love one another. Sacrifice yourselves for your sisters, readily and always. Be kind to them, and never sharp or harsh. Don't nurse resentment, but be meek and peaceable.

INDEX